DISASTER ADMINISTRATION

THEORY AND PRACTICE

DISASTER ADMINISTRATION

THEORY AND PRACTICE

(Text Book for all Disaster Management Courses)

DR. S.L. GOEL

Professor of Public Administration (Retd.)
Panjab University, Chandigarh
Emeritus Fellow, University Grants Commission,
Editor, The Indian Journal of Public Administration, New Delhi
Former Vice-President, Executive Council, Indian Institute of Public Administration, New Delhi
Former Director, State Bank of India Local Board, Chandigarh
Former Member of UGC, Member Distance Education Council and Member All India Board of Management, AICTE, Ministry of HRD, GOI, New Delhi.
Consultant, National Co-operative Union of India

DEEP & DEEP PUBLICATIONS PVT. LTD.

F-159, Rajouri Garden, New Delhi-110027

DISASTER ADMINISTRATION
Theory snd Practice

ISBN 978-81-8450-176-6

Typeset by S.S. COMPOSERS,
3190, Mohindra Park, Shakur Basti, Delhi-110034.

Printed in India at MAYUR ENTERPRISES,
WZ Plot No. 3, Gujjar Market, Tihar Village, New Delhi-110018.

Published by DEEP & DEEP PUBLICATIONS PVT. LTD.,
F-159, Rajouri Garden, New Delhi-110027.
Phones: 25435369, 25440916
E-mail: ddpbooks@yahoo.co.in • deep98@del3.vsnl.net.in
Showroom:
2/13, Ansari Road, Daryaganj, New Delhi-110002 • Telefax: 23245122

Contents

PREFACE

National disasters are increasing every year. In this very year, that is 2008, there were severe problems of floods in Bihar, Orissa, Maharashtra, Gujarat, Punjab and many other places. Besides climate changes are creating new problems causing disasters. On 19th Oct., 2008 Metro over bridge under construction in Delhi collapsed killing 3 people and injured several.

Besides natural disasters, we are witnessing disasters created by human beings themselves like HIV/AIDs, Slums, Chemical disasters, Epidemics, Ethnic conflicts and violence, Terrorism which is more dangerous than natural disasters as these are of daily occurrences. India — like other countries is facing acute problems of terrorism, ethnic violence causing rift in society and lawlessness. There is a perpetual danger to everyone for his security. Such disasters do not allow the country to flourish. We have not discussed these issues in this book as the purpose of this book is to make the common reader understand the nature of disaster and contribute to lessen the impact of disasters. The topics covered are given in the contents.

All the citizens especially students in schools, colleges and universities must be educated in the art and science of disaster administration so that we can cope with the fury of natural and man-made disasters. Government has to change their policies so that through disaster control, sustainable development becomes a reality.

There is an immediate need for initiating action of various levels by all concerned on this issue in order to streamline and improve our disaster preparedness and response capacities. The issue of communication, flow of information, role clarity of various organizations and agencies involved, networking, involvement of the panchayats and strong interface amongst various government departments, institutions, etc. are equally important.

It is hoped that the book "Disaster Administration: Theory and Practice" would be of great advantage to every one interested in Disaster Prevention, Preparedness and Rehabilitation.

S.L. GOEL

1

Disaster Administration: An Introduction

INTRODUCTION

The word disaster of any kind causes fear, anxiety, nervousness in the minds of the people and hence it is essential to understand the disaster and its underlying causes as well as how to deal with it.

Disaster whether natural or man-made are causing a great loss to all sorts of life—Human beings, animals, plants and resources-buildings, infrastructure and above all cause psychological problems. Disasters are increasing with the move to material civilization, urbanization, industrialization and greed. With this new cult, even natural disasters are occurring because of the disturbances in natural equilibrium caused by the greed and lust of human beings to exploit natural resources to get rich quickly.

"Disasters of all types e.g. earthquakes, floods, accidents, cloud bursts, cyclones, etc. have been occurring since time immemorial. However, their frequency, magnitude and area have increased many times in all parts of the world, in recent times. While natural disasters cannot be controlled with the available advanced knowledge of science and technology, many other disasters are the result of wrong developments or planning in all spheres, be it construction of dams, roads, buildings, factories or industries. We are in a great hurry to accelerate the process of development. But with what result and at what cost? We must also be aware of the greater disaster series awaiting us like AIDS, Accidents, Violence, corruption, frauds, cheating, etc. What has been the result of all these disasters? These have resulted in loss of life, half dead living persons, hunger, poverty, unemployment, disease, etc. These are the scars on the face of humanity in this age of nuclear science and information technology.

The Secretary General of the United Nations in his statement on International Decade for Natural Disaster Reduction has rightly remarked that 'natural disasters, arrest the process of economic development and often set it back by many years'. Restorations and repairs of the fractured infrastructure, particularly, roads, communications, power, irrigation are undoubtedly a daunting task. It also requires substantial resources. The desirability of integrating restoration work in the development plans of the state must be examined. The Planning Commission and the successive Finance Commissions have also emphasized this aspect. A disaster management programme which will address itself of mitigating disasters such as cyclone, floods, landslides and earthquake along the lines of the Drought Prone Area Programme would facilitate the process of integration of restoration work in the Plan.

Carl Sagan in his magnificent, awe inspiring work Cosmos has described human predicament and dilemmas that surround us in the most thought provoking manner: "The earth is a lovely and more or less placid place. Things change, but slowly. We can lead a full life and never personally encounter a natural disaster more violent than a storm. And so we become complacent, relaxed, unconcerned. But in the history of Nature, the record is clear. Worlds have been devastated. Even we humans have achieved the dubious technical distinction of being able to make our own disasters, both intentional and inadvertent. On the landscapes of other planets where the records of the past have been preserved there is abundant evidence of major catastrophes. It is all a matter of time scale. An event that would be unthinkable in a hundred years may be inevitable in a hundred million.

Our lovely blue planet, the Earth, is the only home we know. Venus is too hot. Mars is too cold. But the Earth is just right, a heaven for humans. After all, we evolved here. But our congenial climate may be unstable. We are perturbing our poor planet in serious and contradictory ways. Is there any danger of driving the environment of the earth towards the planetary Hell of Venus or the global ice age of Mars? The simple answer is that nobody knows. The study of the global climate, the comparison of the Earth with other worlds, are subjects in their earliesf stages of development. They are fields that are poorly and grudgingly funded. In our ignorance, we continue to push and pull, to pollute the atmosphere and brighten the land, oblivious of the fact that the long-term consequences are largely unknown.

Meaning: (See Chart 1.1)

The Webster's Dictionary, defines disaster as "any event that overwhelms existing resources to deal with the

CHART 1.1

Damage to Environment and Pollution
Damage of infrastructure
Psychological Disorders
Family dislocation
Disruption of moral life
Casualities
Fear Psychologist
Sacrcity of Food, Medicine, Potable water, etc.
Loss of livelihood
Disaster

event." According to Ministry of Environment and Forest, GOI, "A disaster is a Catastrophic consequence of Natural Phenomena or a combination of Phenomena resulting in injury, loss of life or input in a relatively large scale and some disruption to human activities." Prof. Dilip Kumar Sinha in his Presidential Address to Indian Science Congress, "Coping with Natural disasters: An integrated approach" at Indore in 1991 feels that—In an Indian setting, natural disasters whatever be the kind, are seldom found to be stingy in respect of their impact and aftermath, Ravages wrought by them are invariably pervasive; populations whatever be the nature become victims; settlements, human and other, are disrupted; buildings and structures are dismantled, often razed to the ground; mental frame is found reeling heavily; environment in its entirety becomes thus terribly degraded. As mitigation and alleviation of miseries stand out to be necessary tasks in the wake of natural disasters, attention to medical care and needs often come as third in order of priority, food and shelter having obviously higher precedence.[1]

Disaster is defined as: ".....a serious disruption of the functioning of a society, causing widespread human, material, or environment losses which exceed the ability of the affected society to cope using its own resource." A disaster is the product of a hazard such as earthquake, flood or windstorm coinciding with a vulnerable situation which might include communities, cities or villages. There are two main components in this definition: hazard and vulnerability. Without vulnerability or hazard there is no disaster. A disaster occurs when hazards and vulnerability meet.[2]

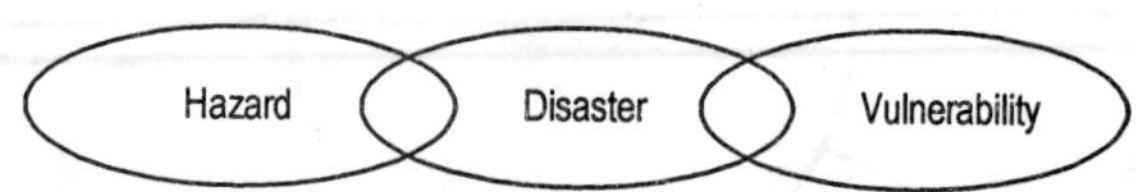

A natural disaster is an event of the nature, which causes sudden disruption to the normal life of a society and causes damage to property and lives, to such an extent, that normal social and economic mechanisms, available to the society, are inadequate to restore normalcy. Viewed in this perspective, a host of natural phenomena constitutes disasters to a society, whether they are related to an occurrence in a micro-environment or not. In macro-terms, the disasters, which cause widespread damage and disruption in India, are drought, flood, cyclone, and earthquakes.

DISTINCTION BETWEEN HAZARD AND DISASTER

Hazard and disaster are closely related. ". . .A hazard is a natural event while the disaster is its consequence. A hazard is a perceived natural event which threatens both life and property. . . a disaster is the realization of this hazard. . ." (John Whittow, Disaster, 1980). Pan American Health Organization in its Scientific Publication No. 575 in 2000 describes the difference very clearly. To quote:

The term "disaster" usually refers to the natural event (e.g., a hurricane or earthquake) in combination with its damaging effects (e.g., the loss of life or destruction of buildings). "Hazard" refers to the natural event, and "vulnerability" to the susceptibility of a population or system (e.g., a hospital, water supply and sewage system, or aspects of infrastructure) to the effects of the hazard. The probability that a particular system or population will be affected by hazards is known as the "risk." Hence, risk is a function of the vulnerability and the hazard, and is expressed as follows:

Risk = Vulnerability × Hazard

Twigg, J. (2001) extracted from Living with Risk. A global review of disaster reduction initiatives 2004 version States "Strictly speaking, there is no such thing as a natural disaster, but there are natural hazards, such as cyclones and earthquakes. The difference between a hazard and a disaster is an important one. A disaster takes place when a community is affected by a hazard (usually defined as an event and even psychological factors that shape peoples that overwhelms that community's capacity to cope). In other words, the impact of the disaster is determined by the extent of a community's vulnerability to the hazard. This vulnerability is not natural. It is the human dimension of disasters, the result of the whole range of economic, social, cultural, institutional, political lives and create the environment that they live in".

Disaster Management Act 2005 defines Disaster management as : "Disaster" means a catastrophe, mishap, calamity or grave occurrence in any area, arising from natural or man-made causes, or by accident or negligence which results in substantial loss of life or human suffering or damage to, and destruction of, property, or damage to, or degradation of environment, and is of such a nature or magnitude as to be beyond the coping capacity of the community of the affected area; "disaster management" means a continuous and integrated process of planning, organising, coordinating and implementing measures which are necessary or expedient for—

(i) prevention of danger or threat of any disaster;
(ii) mitigation or reduction of risk of any disaster or its severity or consequences;
(iii) capacity-building;
(iv) preparedness to deal with any disaster;
(v) prompt response to any threatening disaster situation or disaster;
(vi) assessing the severity or magnitude of effects of any disaster;
(vii) evacuation, rescue and relief; and
(viii) rehabilitation and reconstruction.

The term 'Disaster' owes its origin to the French word 'Desastre' which is the combination of two terms 'des' meaning bad or evil and 'astre' meaning 'star'. The combined expression is 'Bad or Evil Star'. In earlier days a disaster was considered to be the loss due to some unfavourable star.

Disaster is associated with following features:

(1) Disruption to normal pattern of life. Such disruption is usually severe and may also be sudden, unexpected and widespread and thus human beings remain in shock for a long period.

(2) Human effects such as loss of life, livelihood and property, injury, hardship and adverse affects on health—physical as well as mental.
(3) Effects on social structure such as destruction of or damage to infrastructure buildings, communication and other essential services leading to disruption of life and the resources become scarce.
(4) Community needs such as shelter, food, clothing, medical assistance and social care.

A complete definition of disaster may be "an event, concentrated in time and space, which threatens a society or a relatively self-sufficient sub-division of a society with major unwanted consequences as a result of the collapse of precautions which had hitherto been culturally accepted as inadequate" (Turner, 1976).

The world bank operational directive OD 8.50 Emergency Assistance Work system DC, 1989 regards disaster as an extra-ordinary event of limited, duration or strictly speaking a natural event causing serious disruption of countries economy.

Fredic Krimgold in his article: "Overview of the Priority Area Natural Disaster (UN, 1976) regards that a native tendency is to equate natural hazards with natural disasters, the correct notion emerges only when natural disaster and/or hazards are considered in the context of what are caused vulnerabilities:

According to G.F. White, "Disaster is an interaction between people and the nature governed by the co-existent state of adjustment in the human use system and the state of nature and the natural event system".

Luzzari Stefarno in a WHO document defines a disaster as any occurrence causing damage, ecological disruption, loss of human lives, deterioration of health and health services on a scale sufficient to warrant any extra-ordinary intervention from outside the affected community. D.K. Smith in a WMO document defines natural disaster as "catastrophic consequence of natural phenomena or a combination of phenomena resulting in injury, loss of life or input in a relatively large-scale and some disruption to human activities.[3]

Anthony, R. Michaelis has sought to define a natural disaster on the basis of casualties suffered by the people involved: if thousand to one million people be dead or be in immediate danger or death, he would call the event a natural disaster. [4]

Haroid D. Foster has put forward the most comprehensive notion of natural disaster, his scale being built around a social stress rating, derived from individual's loss or a change subsequent to his being involved in a disaster, his is one of few definitions, formally making allowance for the difference between the developed and developing countries so as to arrive at the total stress caused during a disaster.[5] WHO has often considered another phase before the pre-disaster phase and it has been labeled as non-disaster phase; the very titles speak of their import.

Thomas E. Drabek drawing upon extant studies on human responses to disasters, has proposed a rich inventory and this has enabled him to put forward a distinct classification system by disaster phase and system level of response. The disaster phases are preparedness—(1) Planning; (2) Warning, response; (3) Evacuation; (4) Emergency, recovery; (5) Restoration; (6) Reconstruction and mitigation; (7) Hazards perception; and (8) Adjustment. The system levels range from the individual to the international.[6]

The United Nations defines disasters as "The Occurrence of a sudden or major misfortune which disrupts the basic fabric and normal functioning of a society or community".

DISASTER POTENTIAL OF INDIA

India covers an area of 32,87,263 sq. km. extending from snow covered Himalayan heights in the North to the tropical rain forest of the South. In the North, the territory is bounded by the Great Himalayas and stretches southwards tapering off into the Indian ocean between the Bay of Bengal and the Arabian Sea. The main land extends between latitude 8"4' and 37"6' North and longitudes 68.7 and 97.25 East, measuring about 32,000 km from North to South and West to East. The vast land frontier of 15,200 km and coastline of 7,500 km. also has group of islands located both in the Bay of Bengal and the Arabian Sea. Hardly any other country has such a large land mass with such a diverse range of geo-agro-climatic zones. The main land of India comprises of four regions, namely, the Great Mountain Zone, Plains of the Indus, Ganges and the Brahmaputra, the Desert Region, and the Southern Peninsula. The Himalayan range comprises three almost parallel ranges interspread with large plateaus and valleys. The mountain wall extends over a distance of 24,000 km. with a varying width of 240 to 320 km. The plain about 2,400 km. long, are formed by basins of three distinct river systems, viz. the Indus, the Ganges and the Brahmaputra. The desert region is clearly delineated in two parts-Sindh Frontier while the little desert extends between Jaisalmer and Jodhpur upto Punjab. The desert region is inhabited by local communities which have developed their own coping and recovery mechanisms. Between the two deserts is a zone of absolute sterile region, consisting of rocky land cut up by limestones ridges."

India has been traditionally vulnerable to natural disasters on account of its unique geo-climatic conditions. Floods, droughts, cyclones, earthquakes and landslides have been a recurrent phenomena. About 60% of the landmass is prone to earthquakes of various intensities; over 40 million hectares is prone to floods; about 8% of the total area is prone to cyclones and 68% of the area is susceptible to drought. In the decade 1990-2000, an average of about 4344 people lost their lives and about 30 million people were affected by disasters every year. The loss in terms of private, community and public assets has been astronomical.

According to 2001 census, India had a population of 1027 million with 195.02 million housing units. The literacy rate as per 2001 census was 65.38 percent, 75.85 percent for male and 54.16 percent for female. To protect such a large population with low levels of education from the fury of natural hazards is not an easy task. However, local initiatives and the government efforts combined over the years, have tried to reduce risks and build community capacity to deal with emergencies.

At the global level, there has been considerable concern over natural disasters. Even as substantial scientific and material progress is made, the loss of lives and property due to disasters has not decreased. In fact, the human toll and economic losses have mounted. It was in this background that the United Nations General Assembly, in 1989, declared: "The decade 1990-2000 as the International Decade for Natural Disaster Reduction with the objective to reduce loss of lives and property and restrict socio-economic damage through concerted international action, specially in developing countries."

Because of the large geographical size of the country, India often faces natural hazards like floods, cyclones and drought occurring frequently in different parts of the country. At times, some area normally subjected to drought situation have got flooded in certain years. Hazards like earthquakes, hailstorms, avalanches, landslides, etc. occur quite suddenly but they are restricted in their impact in terms of time. The extent of the impact of an earthquake depends on its magnitude, season and time of occurrence.

Indeed, as Kofi Annan, former Secretary General of United Nations, stated at the Programme Forum of the International Decade for Natural Disaster Reduction (IDNDR) held in Geneva, "The humanitarian community does a remarkable job in responding to disaster. But the most important task in the medium and long-term is to strengthen and broaden programmes which reduce the number and cost of disasters in the first place." While we should continue to improve and strengthen our response capacity, we need to engage in working together to build a "global culture of prevention." This means greater efforts to reduce vulnerability to natural hazards in the first place.

The recent occurrence of massive Tsunami on 26.12.2004 has worsened the situation. Though complete prevention of natural disasters is beyond human capabilities, the adverse impact of any disaster on human lives and their livelihoods can be minimized by taking adequate early warning, preparedness and mitigation measures.[7]

TYPES OF DISASTERS (See Chart 1.2)

These can be divided into two types: (i) natural and Man-made disasters.

1. Natural Disasters

(i) Wind-related-Storm, cyclone, tornado, Huricane, Storm surge, Tidal waves.
(ii) Water-related-food, Cloud Burst, Flash flood, Excessive rains, Drought, Communicable diseases.
(iii) Earth-related-Earthquake, Tsunamis, Avalanches, Landslides, Volcanic eruptions.

2. Man-made Disasters

(i) War/battle/hostile enemy actions.
(ii) Arson/sabotage/internal disturbance/riots.
(iii) Accidents of vehicles/trains/aircraft/ships.

FIGURE 1.2

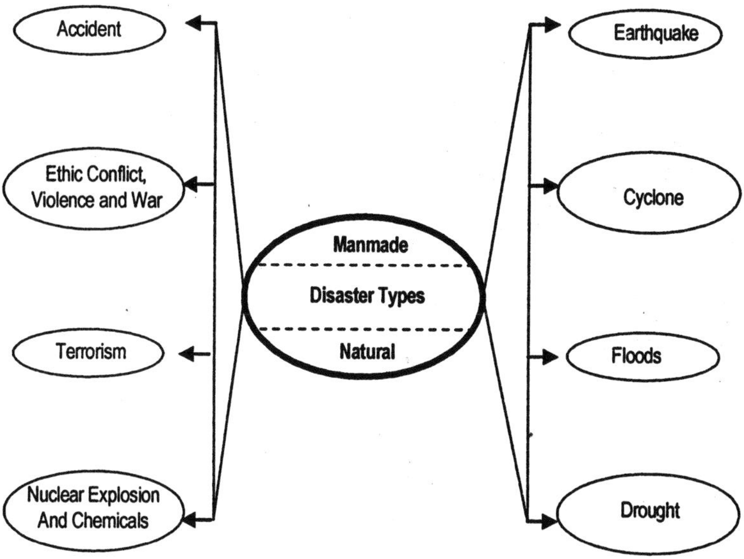

(iv) Industrial accidents/explosion of boilers/gas cylinder or gas chambers/gas leaks.
(v) Fire and Forest fires.
(vi) Nuclear explosion/accidents/radioactive leakages.
(vii) Ecological disasters like deforestation/soil erosion/air/water pollution.
(viii) HIV/AIDS, Life Style diseases.
(ix) Violence.
(x) Collapse of buildings

A High Powered Committee (HPC) of the government of India, in its report, submitted to Government of India in October 2001 mentions the following types of disasters:

I. Water and Climate-related disasters

1. Floods and Drainage Management
2. Cyclones
3. Tornadoes and Hurricanes
4. Hailstorm
5. Cloud Burst
6. Heat Wave and Cold Wave
7. Snow Avalanches
8. Droughts
9. Sea Erosion
10. Thunder and Lighting

II. Geologically-related disasters

1. Landslides and Mudflows
2. Earthquakes
3. Dam Failures/Dam Bursts
4. Mine Fires

III. Chemical, Industrial and Nuclear-related disasters

1. Chemical and Industrial Disasters
2. Nuclear Disasters

IV. Accident-related disasters

1. Forest Fires
2. Urban Fires
3. Mine Flooding
4. Oil Spill
5. Major Building Collapse
6. Serial Bomb Blasts
7. Festival Disasters and Fires
8. Electrical Disasters and Fires
9. Air, Road and Rail Accidents
10. Boat Capsizing
11. Village Fire

V. Biologically-related disasters

1. Biological Disaster and Epidemics
2. Pest Attacks
3. Cattle Epidemics
4. Food Poisoning

VI. Ethnic conflict

VII. Terrorism

Different natural calamities can be distinguished from each other in terms of their nature and extent of their impact. Calamities like earthquakes, hailstorms, avalanches, landslides, etc. occur quite suddenly but they are restricted in their impact in terms of time and space. Similarly, though floods and cyclones occur with some element of warning yet their occurrence is confined in duration. Drought, on the other hand, spans over a much longer time-frame and its adverse impact on the economic activities and life of an area is of a more lasting nature. The measures required to meet the threats posed by different calamities, therefore, differ considerably in terms of disaster preparedness and amelioration of the economic and social life of the affected people.

Natural calamities may be broadly grouped into major and minor types depending upon their potential to cause damage to human life and property. While natural calamities like earth-quakes, droughts, floods and cyclones could be regarded as major, hailstorms, avalanches, landslides, fire accidents, etc. whose impact is localised and intensity of the damage is much less and can be categorised as minor calamities.

Minor calamities like hailstorms, avalanches, landslides and fires also occur without any appreciable degree of forewarning and cause damage to properties and lives. However, areas prone to such disasters also could be identified and certain precautionary measures taken in the context of potential threat requiring general awareness and an ability to relate to a predefined system of appropriate responses on the part of the local administration

TABLE 1.1

Damage due to Natural Disaster in India

Year	*People affected (in lakhs)*	*Houses and Buildings, partially or totally damaged*	*Amount of property damaged/ loss (Crores)*
1965	595.5	2449.878	40.06
1966	550.0	2049.227	30.74
1967	483.4	2919.380	20.57
1968	101.5	242.553	40.63
1990	90.1	782.343	20.41
1991	31.7	1019.930	10.71
1992	242.7	570.696	10.90
1993	190.9	1529.916	20.05
1994	626.5	1051.223	50.80
1995	235.3	2088.355	10.83
1996	549.9	2376.693	40.73
1997	443.2	1103.549	50.43
1998	521.7	1563.405	NA
1999	501.7	3104.064	1020.57
2000	594.34	2736.355	800.00
2001	788.19	864.878	1200.00

Source: Annual Report, NDM Division, Ministry of Agriculture.

Extent: Table 1.1 mentions the losses due to natural disaster from 1965 to 2001. Table 1.2 present the list of some significant earthquake in India. We may mention the recorded losses due to earth quake.

TABLE 1.2

List of Some Significant Earthquake in India

Date	*Place*	*Toll*
1803	Garhwal	200 die
April 4, 1905	Gangra valley (Himachal Pradesh) 8.0 magnitude	20,000 die
July 8, 1918	Assam, 7.6 magnitude	10,000 die
July 2, 1930	Dhubri (Assam) 7.1 magnitude	NA
January 15, 1934	Bihar and Indo-Nepal border, 8.3 magnitude	NA
June 26, 1941	Andaman Islands, 8.1 magnitude	532 die
Oct. 23, 1943	Assam 7.2. magnitude	NA
August 15, 1950	Assam, 8.5 magnitude	NA
July 21, 1956	Anjar (Gujarat) 7.0 magnitude	NA
December 10, 1967	Koyna (Maharashtra) 6.5 magnitude	NA
January 19, 1975	Kinnaur (Himachal Pradesh) 6.2 magnitude	NA
August 21, 1988	Bihar and Indo-Negal border, 6.5 magnitude	1000 die
October 20, 1991	Uttarkanshi (Utter Pradesh) 6.6 magnitude	1500 die
September 30, 1993	Latur and Osmanabad (Maharashtra) 6.3 magnitude	7928 die
May 22, 1997	Jabalpur (M.P.) 6.0 magnitude	40 die
March 29, 1999	Chamboli (UP) 6.8 magnitude	150 die
Januray 20, 2001	Gujarat 6.9 magnitude	13811 die
Dec. 26, 2004	Tsunami A.P. and Tamil Nadu	136132

Source: Compiled from Govt. documents.

CONCLUSION

Disaster Response cannot be handled by Legislation alone. The entire community needs to be aware and part of the process. Adequate Research and Planning is needed to focus on ways to mitigate the impact of Diseases.

Our vision 2020 is to build a safer and secure India through sustained collective effort, synergy of national capacities and people's participation. What looks a dream today will be transformed into reality in the next two decades. This is our goal and we shall strive to achieve this goal with a missionary zeal. The path ahead, which looks difficult today, will become a lot easier as we move along together.

Notes and References

1. Quoted in Indian Science Congress Association, Presidential Address by Prof. Dalip Kumar Sinha, 1991, The Shaping of Indian Science , Indian Science Congress Association, 2003, Vol. III, pp. 1989-2008.
2. GOI, Ministry of Home Affairs, National Disaster Management Division: A Primer For Parliamentarians, New Delhi, pp. 5-6.
3. Quoted in Indian Science Congress Association, Presidential Addresses by Prof. Dilip Kumar Sinha, 1991, The Shaping of Indian Science, Indian Science Congress Association, Presidential Address, 2003, Vol. III, 1982-2003; p. 1729.
4. *Ibid.*
5. *Ibid.*
6. *Ibid.*
7. ICT for Disaster Risk Reduction, Ministry of Home Affairs, National Disaster Management Division, GOI, p. 1.

2

Impact of Disasters on Soci-economic Development

IMPACT OF DISASTERS

Today it is a proven fact that Natural Disasters can happen at any place irrespective of the developed, developing or the least developed status of a country. It can cause massive destruction to the lives and livelihoods of large population and hence, to the national economies. It is experienced that the least developed and developing countries are impacted more severely by large scale natural disasters as their administrative machinery is not efficient and effective to manage disasters (See Chart 2.1)

The impact of natural disasters in term of human and economic losses has risen in recent years, and society in general has become more vulnerable to natural disasters. Those usually most affected by natural and other disasters are the poor and socially disadvantaged groups in developing countries as they are least equipped to cope with them.

Though all disasters are unique in that they affect areas with different levels of vulnerability and with distinct social, health, and economic conditions, there are still similarities between disasters. If recognized, these common factors can be used to optimize the management of health and humanitarian assistance and use of resources (see Table 2.1). The following points should be noted:

CHART 2.1

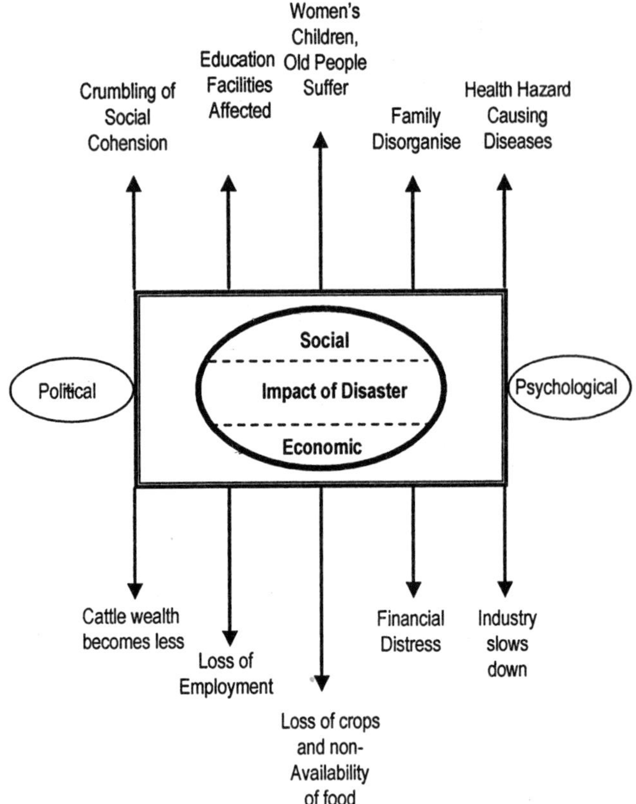

In a matter of minutes an entire country can see its infrastructure destroyed, its economy smashed and its people even deprived of their livelihood. Mankind has been stricken by earthquakes, cyclones, floods, drought and epidemic diseases throughout recorded history. Man's own folly too leaves endless suffering in its wake, and Spaceship Earth carries a menacing burden as it whirls its human crew through time and space, Nuclear weapons, the population explosion and the yawning gulf between rich and poor still trouble our planet until the question arises whether we are

TABLE 2.1

Short-term Effects of Major Disasters

Effects	*Earth-quakes*	*High Winds (without flooding)*	*Tidal waves/flash Floods*	*Slow-onset floods*	*Landslides Lahars*	*Volcanoes/*
1	2	3	4	5	6	7
Deaths*	Many	Few	Many	Few	Many	Many
Severe injuries requiring extensive treatment	Many	Moderate	Few	Few	Few	Few
Increased risk of communicable disease	Potential risk following all major disasters (Probability rising with overcrowding and deteriorating sanitation)					
Damage to health facilities	Severe (structure and equipment)	Severe	Severe but Localized	Severe (equipment only)	Severe but Localized)	Severe (structure and equipment)

(Contd.)

TABLE 2.1 *(Contd.)*

1	*2*	*3*	*4*	*5*	*6*	*7*
Damage to water systems	Severe	Light	Severe	Light	Severe but Localized	Severe
Food Shortage	Rare	Common	Common	Common	Rare	Rare
Major Population Movements	(may occur due to economic and logistic factors) Rare may occur in heavily damaged urban areas)		Common (generally limited)			

Source: GOI, Ministry of Home Affairs, Potential lethal impact in absence of preventive measure.

not fast approaching the day of some vast and final catastrophe."[1]

Whether disasters are of natural origin or man-made, their effects in a country's life can be detected for months, and sometimes even years. It is therefore essential that any support operation be designed and implemented with a long-term perspective.[2]

Disaster whether natural or man-made are causing a great loss to all sorts of life — human beings, animals, plants and resources—buildings, infrastructure and above all cause psychological problems. Disasters are increasing with the move to material civilization, urbanization, industrialization and greed. With this new cult, even natural disasters are occurring because of the disturbances in natural equilibrium caused by the greed and lust of human beings to exploit natural resources to get rich quickly.

"Disasters of all types, e.g. earthquakes, floods, accidents, cloud bursts, cyclones, etc. have been occurring since time immemorial. However, their frequency, magnitude and area have increased many times in all parts of the world in recent times. While natural disasters cannot be controlled with the available advanced knowledge of science and technology, many other disasters are the result of wrong developments or planning in all spheres, be it construction of dams, roads, buildings, factories or industries. We must also be aware of the greater disaster series awaiting us like AIDS, corruption, frauds, cheating terrorism violence, etc. What has been the result of all these disasters? These have resulted in loss of life, half dead living persons, hunger, poverty, unemployment, disease, etc. These are the scars on the face of humanity in this age of nuclear science and information technology.

M. Chakraborty in his article, "Disaster Management: A case of Latur Earthquake" mentions that a natural disaster is a condition of the environment. Huge amount of destruction is caused by such disasters as, property damage, injuries and death, or a long-term socio-economic consequence, outcoming from the event. Mankind lives under a worsening threat of such disasters happening at any time due to any natural phenomenon. Disasters may last for a few minutes or they may even extend for years in which they leave behind only a devastated landscape. Earthquakes are also among such disasters when somewhere below the ground, the joints of two rock masses, locked together under tremendous tension, rupture. The movement may be slight but the energy released is so large that it resembles a bomb explosion and the whole surface tears up with a jerk. With this, all structures like houses, crumble down and after which only heaps of rubbles are left.

Nagapattinam in his article, "The Waves that Developed" in *India Today* clearly explain that when the sea parted off the coast of Indonesia, the raging water roared with a medieval echo. Rising from the floor of the ocean in gigantic waves, it robbed nations of their land, families of their loves ones and towns of their identity. White shrouds in mass graves sometimes with a solitary wreath, heartbroken parents clutching the clammy hands of children long dead, hollow eyes surveying heaps of broken homes and desolate relief workers with their mouths covered, trying desperately to escape the stench of death. The Sumatra quake sent huge waves crashing into coastal areas, killing tens of thousands of people. While Indonesia was the worst hit, India suffered massive damage in terms of lives and property.

The struggle against disasters is still a matter of development. As with all other misfortunes that plague humanity, such as disease and ignorance, disasters strike hardest at those who most lack any defence. But as in other fields it is on these same people that we can most rely. Just as we have observed communities actively interesting themselves in their own development ever since international aid movements have learnt to see problems through the eyes of the underdeveloped themselves, so the strangers who first arrive on the scene of a disaster invariably find the victims, not sitting passively by and waiting for help, but already busily engaged in making sure that daily life goes on. It is among these reserves of goodwill and community spirit that we may perhaps find the greatest fund of human resources for reconstruction.[3]

Natural disasters strike countries, both developed and developing, all over the world. Every year, more than twenty natural disasters occur throughout the globe. In last two decades, disasters have claimed more than three billion lives and affected about one billion people. The frequency of natural disasters is many times more in Asia and pacific region. India, like many other developing countries, is affected by different types of disasters every year, such as earthquakes, floods, droughts, cyclones, snowstorms, hailstorms, etc. These disasters hinder many developmental projects as huge amounts have to be diverted for relief and recovery.[4]

A natural hazard is an event of nature, which causes sudden disruption to the normal life of a society and causes damage to life and property, to such an extent that normal, social and economic mechanisms available to the society are inadequate to restore normalcy. Viewed in this manner, a host of natural phenomena causes disasters to a society, whether they are related to an occurrence in micro-environment or not. In macro-terms, the hazards, which cause widespread damage and disruption in India, are floods, cyclones, earthquakes and landslides.

The past decade has witnessed an extraordinary increase in the number and extent of natural disasters. As Kofi Annan, Secretary General of the United Nations, pointed out, "The facts are startling. The costs of weather-related disasters in 1998 exceeded the costs of all such disasters in the decade of the 1980s. In the Caribbean, the hurricanes designated George and Mitch Miued more than 13,000 people, with Mitch being the deadliest atlantic storm in 200 years. Major floods hit India, Nepal, Bangladesh and much of East Asia, with thousands killed. Two-thirds of Bangladesh was inundated for months, leaving millions homeless. There were three times as many great natural hazards in the 1990s as in the 1960s, while disaster costs increased more than nine-fold in the same period."[5]

"The humanitarian community does a remarkable job in responding to disasters. But the most important task in the medium and long-term is to strengthen and broaden programmes which reduce the number and cost of disasters in the first place." While we should continue to improve and strengthen our response capacity, we need to engage in working together to build a "global culture of prevention." This means greater efforts to reduce vulnerability to natural hazards in the first place.

As we approach the beginning of a new millennium, the IDNDR is proved to have contributed with all its partners world-wide to fostering a "global culture of prevention" for the 21st Century. To build on the progress achieved during the IDNDR, we have to act decisively, so that disaster reduction becomes an essential element of government policies. Recalling the Geneva Mandate adopted at the IDNDR Programme Forum, we have to adopt and implement policy measures at the international, regional, national and local levels aimed at reducing the vulnerability of our societies to natural disasters. These measures should have as main objectives the establishment of hazard resistant communities, the protection of people from the threat of disasters, and the safeguarding of our natural and economic resources and of our social well-being.[6]

K. Rajan suggests the following adversities which befall on people and the area. (See Chart 2.2)

* Loss of crops and availability of essentials like food and agricultural commodities;
* Loss of employment opportunities in the area where natural Disaster occurs and particularly on rural employment;
* Problems of health and diseases arising both from insufficient availability of the basic necessities causing malnourishment, hunger, etc. or on the availability of good and hygienic drinking water;
* Financial distress caused to the farming community and those dependent on land which affect their ability to withstand hard conditions immediately following the occurrence of the natural disaster but also importantly, their ability to recover well enough before the next cropping season and take full advantage of normal conditions which may prevail;
* Impact on industrial sector due to loss of production of raw materials, reduce generation of power, etc.; and

CHART 2.2

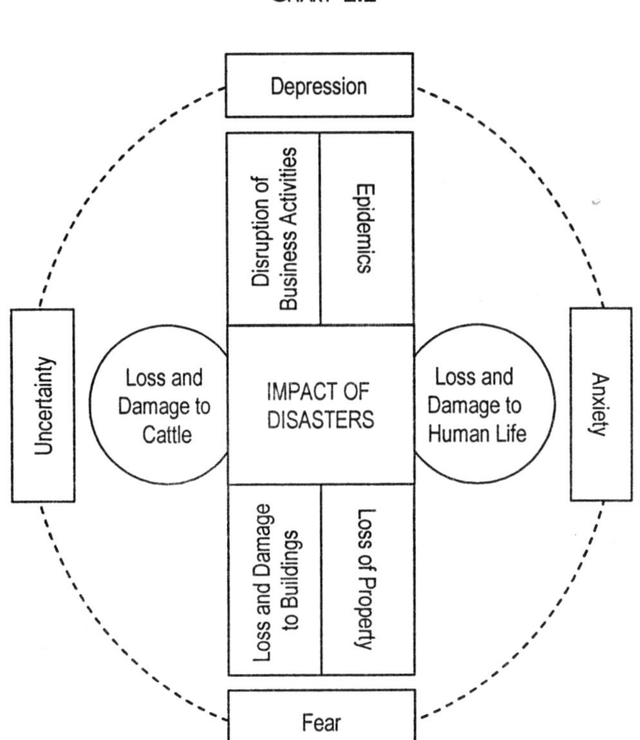

* Lastly, the impact of the disaster on the cattle wealth.

V. Suresh rightly feels that Natural disasters, which damage national economies and produce hardships for large sections of the population, are one of the single largest concerns for most nations. Human settlements are frequently affected by natural disasters—earthquake, floods, hurricanes, cyclones, landslides, sea erosions—which take a heavy toll on human lives, destroy buildings and infrastructure and have far reaching economic and social consequences for communities.[7]

Ashok Pahwa has rightly said, "Natural hazards are not new to the earth system. Like natural resources, they have been, and are, a part of biosphere and eco-systems. It is the human interventions, its endeavours towards development, that these hazards turn into disasters, causing enormous devastation to the life and property of the nations. The extent and frequency of damage, that is being caused by these extreme events, has raised concerns allover the world resulting into declaration of present decade (1990s) as international Decade for Natural Disaster reduction."[8]

Bhagat Singh has suggested the ways to reduce its serious effects while occurrence of these natural disasters cannot be prevented altogether, their adverse impact can be reduced substantially—by undertaking various preparedness and mitigation measures by community involvement. Minimizing the loss of precious human life is the first priority in disaster management. Significant achievement has been made in designing of disaster resistant houses and inventing quality building materials to withstand the fury of natural disasters. It is gratifying to note that HUDCO has given a lead by taking a number of initiatives to propagate these designs as well as materials among the vulnerable community besides imparting training to the artisans and masons through their building centers.[9]

Earthquakes, floods, drought, cyclones, accidents, AIDS are major Types of disaster phenomenon which occurred in the South-East Asia Region, India is a large country and has had more than its share of major natural hazards like drought, floods, earthquakes and cyclones throughout its history of civilization. Naturally, the country developed its own practices and strategies for coping with the various natural calamities. Since independence in 1947, India has developed a nationwide relief administration where a lead role of the State Governments is envisaged.[10]

V. Thiruppugazh and Sudhir Kumar in their article, "E-Governance And Disaster Management" in the Silver symposium of Institute of Rural Management, Anand (Gujarat) rightly stated that in recent years, link between disaster and development is being established by the development community as disasters not only claim lives and destroy social networks but also eat away the development result and pushes back the society and country by several months or years. Hence amalgamation of the Disaster Management with Development Plan/interventions is the key for stable, equitable and sustainable growth and hence poverty reduction. Development should be such that it saves from disaster. "Development should not be such that it itself becomes disaster". (See Chart 2.3)

Shivraj Patil, Minister of Home Affairs has rightly said that the increasing incidents of disasters have been hampering poverty reduction, environmental protection and sustainable development. Disasters wipe out years of development and consumer resources that could have been used for development and social welfare of the people. Disasters and poverty compound each other in vicious cycles.

The following can be the impact of disasters:

1. People, loss of life.
2. Personal health, injury or disease.
3. Damage, destruction of property.
4. Damage, destruction of infrastructure, public service systems.
5. Damage, destruction of environment.
6. Damage, destruction of crops.
7. Disruption, loss of production.
8. Disruption, loss of essential services.
9. Disruption, loss of national infrastructure.
10. Disruption to governmental process, systems.
11. Loss to national, local economies.
12. Disruption, loss of community or lifestyle.
13. Sociological and psychological consequences.

Disasters when occur, have a severe impact on all sections of the society. But globally, it is observed that it is certain sections who are more susceptible. These vulnerable sections lack resources and are deprived of basic necessities, that expose them to the adverse effects. Preparedness activity, is to be holistic that takes into consideration, the hazards for which vulnerable are exposed to, existing resources, capacities and capabilities and attempt to harness their potentials. They need to be integrated in the overall disaster management process. The general tendency is to overlook the contribution of vulnerable groups and consider them more as victims.

Natural Disaster arrest the process of economic development and often set it back by many years. Restorations and repair of the fractured infrastructure, particularly, roads, communications, power, irrigation are undoubtedly a daunting task. It also requires substantial resources. The desirability of integrating restoration work in the development plans of the State must be examined. The Planning Commission and the successive Finance Commissions have also emphasized this aspect. A disaster management programme which will address itself to mitigating disasters such as cyclone, floods, landslides and earthquake along the lines of the Drought Prone Area Programme would facilitate the process of integration of restoration work in the Plan. Such a programme may include preventive precautionary measures and specific projects schemes for Earthquake and Cyclone-prone area.

Disaster Management has to be a multi-disciplinary and pro-active approach in order to tackle socio-economic issues. Besides various measures for putting in place institutional and policy framework, disaster prevention, mitigation and preparedness enunciated earlier and initiatives being taken by the Central and state Governments, the community, civil society organisations and Media also have a key role to play in achieving our goal of moving together, towards a safer India. The message being put across is that, in order to move towards safer and sustainable national development, development projects should be sensitive towards disaster mitigation.

Our mission is vulnerability reduction to all types of hazards, be it natural or man-made. This is not an easy task to achieve, keeping in view the vast population, and the multiple natural hazards to which this country is exposed. However, if we are firm in our conviction and resolve that the Government and the people of this country are not prepared to pay the price in terms of massive casualties and economic losses, the task, though difficult, is achievable and we shall achieve.

We have taken the first few but significant steps towards vulnerability reduction, putting in place prevention and mitigation measures and preparedness for a rapid and professional response. With a massive awareness generation campaign and building up of capabilities as well as institutionalization of the entire mechanism through a techno-legal and techno-financial framework, we are gradually moving in the direction of sustainable development.

Our vision 2020 is to build a safer and secure India through sustained collective effort, synergy of national capacities and people's participation. What looks a dream today will be transformed into reality in the next two decades. This is our goal and we shall strive to achieve this goal with a missionary zeal. The path ahead, which looks difficult today, will become a lot easier as we move along together.

Community awareness forms the basic crux of present day disaster management. The prime objective is to raise the awareness levels, knowledge base of the community to make them alert, self-reliant and cope with the consequences. People have coping strategies that they derive from the past experience. The communities possess the capacity and strength arising out of previous experiences in facing emergencies. This needs to be harnessed. The awareness is required to enable the community understand the impact of disaster, efforts they need to put to reduce its impact and save their lives and property.[11]

CONCLUSION

Country's high vulnerability to a wide array of disaster requires a systematic, planned and professional approach at all levels. But no one can beat us when it comes to not doing right things at right moment. We, as a nation, are notorious for having the best databases but being the worst managers in almost all fields and disaster management is no exception. India has the National Hazard Vulnerability. Atlas that has exhaustive data on every possible hazard that threatens each and every district of the country. We also have plans to tackle disaster situations. But when it comes calling we are found groping in the dark.

Every tragedy leaves us painfully aware that we need to tighten our belts but every time we don't learn the lessons and it takes another disaster to shake us from slumber. And it is not the government alone that has to be blamed for it as we must work together collectively as individuals and institutions. The civil society at large is responsible for the ills we have. It is aptly said that we get the systems we deserve.

Given the fact that almost all the districts of the country are prone to at least one major disaster and 139 districts are multi-hazard prone it is ironic that the country does not have Disaster Management Plans at national, state district and sub-district levels.

In the year 2005, Government of India has enacted National Disaster Management Act and National Disaster Management Authority (NDMA) was established. The aim of this Act is to establish an institutionalized mechanism for management of disasters. Earlier, the disaster management was relief centric with a complete paradigm shift from relief centric to prevention, mitigation and preparedness approach so that the effect of disasters can be mitigated/minimized.

The United Nations Disaster Relief Office (UNDRO) defines Disaster Preparedness as "a series of measures designed to organize and facilitate timely and effective rescue, relief and rehabilitation operations in cases of disaster. Measures of preparedness include among others, setting up disaster relief machinery, formulations of emergency relief plans, training of specific groups (and vulnerable communities) to undertake rescue and relief, stock piling supplies and earmarking funds for relief operations"

In May 1994, a major Conference of the IDNDR programme was held which brought, out a plan of action for disaster reduction called the Yokohama Strategy. It made a case for an accelerated implementation of a Plan of Action with development of a global culture of prevention as a key component of the integrated approach to disaster reduction. The strategy emphasized on the need to increase awareness on the importance of disaster reduction policies, support to states from the international community and evolving an integrated approach to disaster management in all spheres.

The Yokohama Strategy and Plan for Action for a Safer World vehemently propagated a comprehensive prevention, mitigation and preparedness strategy along with developing a culture of prevention, formulating and maintaining preparedness and response plans at the National, State and District levels, adopting a policy of self-reliance in each vulnerable area, and enhancing the capabilities of those involved at all levels through education and training. It also emphasized the necessity of identifying and strengthening the existing centres of excellence to improve disaster prevention, reduction and mitigation capabilities. The IDNDR was to concentrate on sustained international and multi-disciplinary commitment for disaster prevention through focusing on hazard, vulnerability and risk assessment, disaster prevention and sustainable development, effective early warning, sharing of knowledge and transfer of technology.

The standard of living of people depends mainly on socio-economic development. Therefore, there is a need of system which can bring back the socio-economic development in case it is disturbed by disasters.

Hari Singh in his article, "Faulty System and Poor Response: Technology as a Tool For Disaster Management" in the *Daily Tribune* (February 9, 2001) that despite management system is existing, there is no point in boasting about our information technology revolution. We have hardly used IT power for the service of the people. It needs to be realized that information technology has made today's statecraft and politico-economic management virtually outdated. It is, therefore, necessary to shed the old mindset. It is not the people but the system, the persons at the helm and the poor standard of governance which have invariably failed the nation. This has once again been proved by the way the people, here and abroad, have responded, to one of the biggest disasters ever to hit the country in the wake of the devastating earthquake in Gujarat.

However, nothing can work unless the government moves in the right direction and reforms itself by evolving community-based participatory structures and subjects itself to strict accountability.

Through the decade of the 90s we are determined to reach a higher plateau of global awareness of the suffering and damages due to natural disasters and to put in place actions, both possible and necessary, to reduce these human and economic losses. But it will take a major effort on the part of all disaster-prone countries—that is all of our countries—to bring this about. The IDNDR provides an opportunity and a framework for international cooperation. For the sake of the people of the world, let us work together to make it happen.

All the countries of the world must work together to ensure better disaster administration.

Notes and References

1. Christane Viedma, Disaster Alert, *World Health*, June 1978, p. 14.
2. J. Oetio Espiniza, Responding to Disasters, in *World Helath*, Nov.-Dec. 1991, p. 28.
3. Christiane Videma, *op. cit.*, p. 17.
4. M. Wadhwani, Director, Indian Institute of Public Administration, Foreward, quoted in Vinod K. Sharma, *Disaster Management*, New Delhi, IIPA, 1999.
5. R.K. Celley and T.N. Gupta, Dimensions of Natural Disaster Management in India, *Shelter*, Oct. 12, 1992.
6. Phillips, and Boulle, Message, in *Shelter*, Dec. 13, 1999.
7. K.Rajan, Natural Disaster Management in National Development—An Indian Perspective quoted in Vinod K. Sharma, *Disaster Management*, IIPA, New Delhi, 1999, p. 26.
8. V. Suresh, Message Towards a Safer Millennium in *Shelter*, Dec. 13, 1999.
9. Ashok Pahava, *Ibid.*
10. Bhagat Singh, *Ibid.*
11. IDNDR, Indian Experiences and Initiative, p. 3.

3

Organisation for Disaster Administration

ORGANISATION AT INTERNATIONAL LEVEL[1]

As we approach the twenty-first century, population growth, ecological damage, rapid industrialization and socio-economic imbalances make the risk of major disasters around the world higher than ever. We need not, however, be fatalistic about the vagaries of nature. To tackle disasters we have developed organizations at international, national and local levels. However, these are not functioning well in developing countries. (See Chart 3.1)

International Level—The IDNDR Secretariat, located in Geneva, is part of the UN Department of Humanitarian Affairs. The IDNDR Scientific and Technical Committee is an advisory body with experts in economics, social sciences, engineering, public health, industry, geology, meteorology, etc. A group of well-known personalities, the Special High-Level Council, promotes global awareness of disaster reduction. A UN inter-agency group works regularly with the IDNDR Secretariat, as well as a contact group of Geneva-based diplomatic missions.

IDNDR publishes a quarterly magazine, *STOP Disasters*, and conducts a promotional campaign on the second Wednesday of each October, designated as the International Day for Natural Disaster Reduction.

Chart 3.1

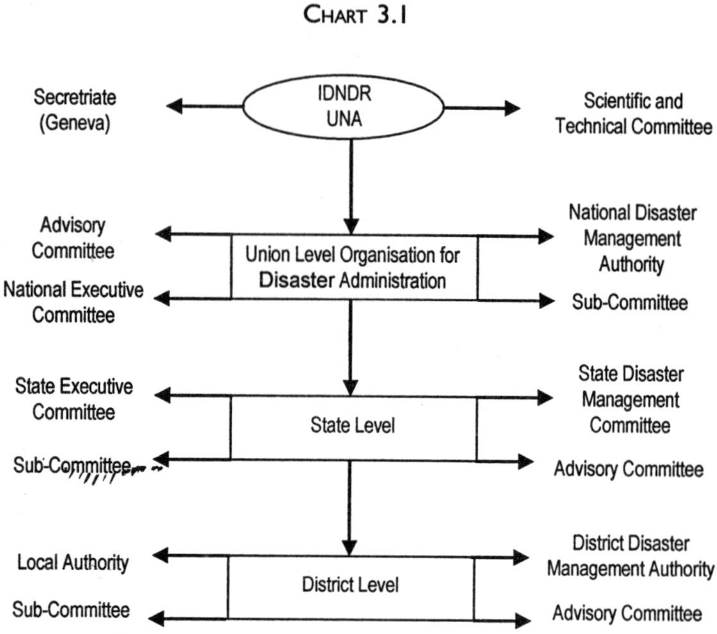

YOKOHAMA STRATEGY AND PLAN OF ACTION FOR A SAFER WORLD

World Conference on Natural Disaster Reduction on Guidelines for Natural Disaster Prevention, Preparedness and Mitigation in Yokohama, Japan, 23-27 May 1994 resolved that we, the States Members of the United Nations and other States, having met at the World Conference on Natural Disaster Reduction, in the city of Yokohama, Japan, from 23 May to 27 May 1994, in partnership with non-governmental organizations, and with the participation of international organizations, the scientific community, business, industry and the media, deliberating within the framework of the International Decade for Natural Disaster Reduction, expressing our deep concern for the continuing human suffering and disruption of development caused by natural disasters.

The adopted Yokohama Strategy and related Plan of Action for the rest of the Decade and beyond:

A. Will note that each country has the sovereign responsibility to protect its citizens from natural disasters;
B. Will give priority attention to the developing countries, in particular the least developed, land-locked countries and the small island developing states;
C. Will develop and strengthen national capacities and capabilities and where appropriate, national legislation for natural and other disaster prevention, mitigation and preparedness, including the mobilization of non-governmental organizations and participation of local communities; and
D. Will promote and strengthen sub-regional, regional and international cooperation in activities to prevent, reduce and mitigate natural and other disasters, with particular emphasis on:
   - Human and institutional capacity-building and strengthening;
   - Technology sharing, the collection, the dissemination and the utilization of information; and
   - Mobilization of resources.

IDNDR works through IDNDR National Committee and Focal Points which exists in 138 countries. The IDNDR Secretariat, located in Geneva, is part of the UN Departemnt of humanitarian Affairs. The IDNDR Scientific and Technical Committee is an advisory body with experts in economics, social sciences engineering, public health, industry, geology, meteorology, etc. A group of well-known personalities, the Special High Level Council, promotes global awareness of disaster reduction. A UN inter-agency group works regularly with the IDNDR Secretariat, as well as a contact group of Geneva-based diplomatic missions.

II. ORGANISATION FOR DISASTER MANAGEMENT AT UNION LEVEL

The subject of disaster management does not find mention directly in any of the three lists, i.e. Union, State and Concurrent list in the 7th Schedule of the Constitution. However, the State Governments are provided financial assistance for meeting expenditure on identified natural calamities on the basis of the recommendations of the Finance Commission. In order to ensure that the assistance is used only for calamity relief, a Calamity Relief Fund has been constituted by each state, where annual assistance is credited and utilized on the basis of guidelines issued by the Union Ministry of Finance.

The two entries in the State List that are remotely related to the subject of disaster management are entry 14, which deals with agriculture, including protection against pests and plant diseases, and entry 17 which deals with water, including water supply, drainage and embankments. The High Powered Committee, strongly felt that this is grossly inadequate, and that Disaster Management needs to be included in the Seventh Schedule of the Constitution under whichever lists is felt most appropriate.

However, the legislation on disaster management has been related to entry 23 (Social Security and Social Insurance) in the Concurrent List of the Constitution and the States would also be able to enact their own legislations on the subject. In fact, the States of Gujarat and Bihar have already enacted their respective disaster management legislations.

Recently—Disaster Management Act has been passed only in 2005 which specifies the role of Union, State and District administration in planning and management of Disasters. There is no enactment either of the Union or of any State Government to deal with the management of disaster of all types in a comprehensive manner. The Environment (Protection) Act, 1986 which was enacted for the 'protection and improvement of environment and the prevention of hazards to human beings, other living creatures, plants and property'. The Ministry of Environment and Forests prepared and published the Rules on

'Emergency Planning, Preparedness and Response for Chemical Accidents in 1996 only'. These rules pertain to toxic and hazardous chemicals, and provide a reference mechanism for the Central, State, district and local levels.

The main provisions of the Disaster Management Act are:

(i) Union Level

1. The National Disaster Management Authority:

(A) Composition, Tenure and Conditions of Service

(a) The National Authority consists of the Chairperson and such number of other members, not exceeding nine, as may be prescribed by the Central Government and, unless the rules otherwise provide, the National Authority shall consist of the following:

(b) The Prime Minister of India is the Chairperson of the National Authority, *ex officio;*

(c) Other members, not exceeding nine, to be nominated by the Chairperson of the National Authority.

(d) The Chairperson of the National Authority may designate one of the members nominated to be the Vice-Chairperson of the National Aurhority.

(B) Powers and Functions: Powers and Functions of National Authority

(1) Subject to the provisions of this Act, the National Authority has the responsibility for laying down the policies, plans and guidelines for disaster management for ensuring timely and effective response to disaster.

2. The National Authority may:

(a) lay down policies on disaster management;

(b) approve the National Plan;

(c) approve plans prepared by the Ministries or Departments of the Government of India in accordance with the National Plan;

(d) lay down guidelines to be followed by the State Authorities in drawing up the State Plan;

(e) lay down guidelines to be followed by the different Ministries or Departments of the Government of India for the purpose of integrating the measures for prevention of disaster or the mitigation of its effects in their development plans and projects;

(f) coordinate the enforcement and implementation of the policy and plan for disaster management;

(g) recommend provision of funds for the purpose of mitigation;

(h) provide such support to other countries affected by major disasters as may be determined by the Central Government;

(i) take such other measures for the prevention of disaster, or the mitigation, or preparedness and capacity building for dealing with the threatening disaster situation or disaster as it may consider necessary; and

(j) lay down broad policies and guidelines for the functioning of the National Institute of Disaster Management.

(3) The Chairperson of the National Authority shall, in the case of emergency, have power to exercise all or any of the powers of the National Authority but exercise of such powers shall be subject to *ex-post facto* ratification by the National Authority.

(ii) State Level

1. State Disaster Management Authority

(A) Establishment of State Disaster Management Authority

(1) Every State Government shall establish a State Disaster Management Authority for the State with such name as may be specified in the notification of the State Government.

(2) A State Authority shall consist of the Chairperson and such number of other members, not exceeding nine, as

may be prescribed by the State Government and, unless the rules otherwise provide, the State Authority shall consist of the following members, namely:

(a) the Chief Minister of the State, who shall be Chairperson, *ex officio;*
(b) other members, not exceeding eight, to be nominated by the Chairperson of the State Authority; and
(c) the Chairperson of the State Executive Committee, *ex officio.*

(3) The Chairperson of the State Authority may designate one of the members nominated under clause (b) of sub-section (2) to be the Vice-Chairperson of the State Authority.

(4) The Chairperson of the State Executive Committee shall be the Chief Executive Officer of the State Authority, *ex officio*:

Provided that in the case of a Union territory having Legislative Assembly, except the Union territory of Delhi, the Chief Minister shall be the Chairperson of the Authority established under this section and in case of other Union territories, the Lieutenant Governor or the Administrator shall be the Chairperson of that Authority:

Provided further that the Lieutenant Governor of the Union territory of Delhi shall be the Chairperson and the Chief Minister thereof shall be the Vice-Chairperson of the State Authority.

(5) The term of office and conditions of service of members of the State Authority shall be such as may be prescribed.

(B) Powers and Functions of State Authority

(1) Subject to the provisions of this Act, a State Authority shall have the responsibility for laying down policies and plans for disaster management in the State.

(2) Without prejudice to the generality of provisions contained in sub-section (1), the State Authority may—

(a) lay down the State disaster management policy;
(b) approve the State Plan in accordance with the guidelines laid down by the National Authority;
(c) approve the disaster management plans prepared by the departments of the Government of the State;
(d) lay down guidelines to be followed by the departments of the Government of the State for the purposes of integration of measures for prevention of disasters and mitigation in their development plans and projects and provide necessary technical assistance therefor;
(e) coordinate the implementation of the State Plan;
(f) recommend provision of funds for mitigation and preparedness measures;
(g) review the development plans of the different departments of the State and ensure that prevention and mitigation measures are integrated therein; and
(h) review the measures being taken for mitigation, capacity building and preparedness by the departments of the Government of the State and issue such guidelines as may be necessary.

(3) The Chairperson of the State Authority shall, in the case of emergency, have power to exercise all or any of the powers of the State Authority but the exercise of such powers shall be subject to *ex-post facto* ratification of the State Authority.

(iii) District Level

(A) Constitution of District Disaster Management Authority

(1) Every State Government shall, as soon as may be after issue of notification under sub-section (1) of section 14, by notification in the Official Gazette, establish a District Disaster Management Authority for every district in the State with such name as may be specified in that notification.

(2) The District Authority shall consist of the Chairperson and such number of other members, not exceeding seven, as may be prescribed by the State Government, and unless the rules otherwise provide, it shall consist of the following, namely:

(a) the Collector or District Magistrate or Deputy Commissioner, as the case may be, of the district who shall be Chairperson, *ex officio;*

(b) the elected representative of the local authority who shall be the co-Chairperson, *ex officio*:
Provided that in the Tribal Areas, as referred to in the Sixth Schedule to the Constitution, the Chief Executive Member of the district council of autonomous district, shall be the co-Chairperson, *ex officio;*

(c) the Chief Executive Officer of the District Authority, *ex officio;*

(d) the Superintendent of Police, *ex officio;*

(e) the Chief Medical Officer of the district, *ex officio;* and

(f) not exceeding two other district level officers, to be appointed by the State Government.

(3) In any district where zila parishad exists, the Chairperson thereof shall be the co-Chairperson of the District Authority.

(4) The State Government shall appoint an officer not below the rank of Additional Collector or Additional District Magistrate or Additional Deputy Commissioner, as the case may be, of the district to be the Chief Executive Officer of the District Authority to exercise such powers and perform such functions as may be prescribed by the State Government and such other powers and functions as may be delegated to him by the District Authority.

(B) Powers and Functions of District Authority

(1) The District Authority shall act as the district planning, coordinating and implementing body for disaster management and take all measures for the purposes of

disaster management in the district in accordance with the guidelines laid down by the National Authority and the State Authority.

(2) Without prejudice to the generality of the provisions of sub-section (1), the District Authority may—

(i) prepare a disaster management plan including district response plan for the district;

(ii) coordinate and monitor the implementation of the National Policy, State Policy, National Plan, State Plan and District Plan;

(iii) ensure that the areas in the district vulnerable to disasters are identified and measures for. the prevention of disasters and the mitigation of its effects are undertaken by the departments of the Government at the district level as well as by the local authorities;

(iv) ensure that the guidelines for prevention of disasters, mitigation of its effects, preparedness and response measures as laid down by the National Authority and the State Authority are followed by all departments of the Government at the district level and the local authorities in the district;

(v) give directions to different authorities at the district level and local authorities to take such other measures for the prevention or mitigation of disasters as may be necessary;

(vi) lay down guidelines for prevention of disaster management plans by the department of the Government at the districts level and local authorities in the district;

(vii) monitor the implementation of disaster management plans prepared by the Departments of the Government at the district level;

(viii) lay down guidelines to be followed by the Departments of the Government at the district level for purposes of integration of measures for prevention of disasters and mitigation in their development plans and projects and provide necessary technical assistance therefore;

(ix) monitor the implementation of measures referred to in clause (viii);

(x) review the state of capabilities for responding to any disaster or threatening disaster situation in the district and give directions to the relevant departments or authorities at the district level for their upgradation as may be necessary;

(xi) review the preparedness measures and give directions to the concerned departments at the district level or other concerned authorities where necessary for bringing the preparedness measures to the levels required for responding effectively to any disaster or threatening disaster situation;

(xii) organise and coordinate specialised training programmes for different levels of officers, employees and voluntary rescue workers in the district;

(xiii) facilitate community training and awareness programmes for prevention of disaster or mitigation with the support of local authorities, governmental and non-governmental organisations;

(xiv) set-up, maintain, review and upgrade the mechanism for early warnings and dissemination of proper information to public;

(xv) prepare, review and update district level response plan and guidelines;

(xvi) coordinate response to any threatening disaster situation or disaster;

(xvii) ensure that the Departments of the Government at the district level and the local authorities prepare their response plans in accordance with the district response plan;

(xviii) lay down guidelines for, or give direction to, the concerned Department of the Government at the district level or any other authorities within the local limits of the district to take measures to respond effectively to any threatening disaster situation or disaster;

(xix) advise, assist and coordinate the activities of the Government at the district level, statutory governmental and non-governmental organisations in the disaster management; of the Departments bodies and other districts engaged;

(xx) coordinate with, and give guidelines to, local authorities in the district to ensure that measures for the prevention or mitigation of threatening disaster situation or disaster in the district are carried out promptly and effectively;

(xxi) provide necessary technical assistance or give advice to the local authorities in the district for carrying out their functions;

(xxii) review development plans prepared by the Departments of the Government at the district level, statutory authorities or local authorities with a view to make necessary provisions therein for prevention of disaster or mitigation;

(xxiii) examine the construction in any area in the district and, if it is of the opinion that the standards for the prevention of disaster or mitigation laid down for such construction is not being or has not been followed, may direct the concerned authority to take such action as may be necessary to secure compliance of such standards;

(xxiv) identify buildings and places which could, in the event of any threatening disaster situation or disaster, be used as relief centers or camps and make arrangements for water supply and sanitation in such buildings or places;

(xxv) establish stockpiles of relief and rescue materials or ensure preparedness to make such materials available at a short notice;

(xxvi) provide information to the State Authority relating to different aspects of disaster management;

(xxvii) encourage the involvement of non-governmental organisations and voluntary social-welfare institutions working at the grassroots level in the district for disaster management;

{xxviii} ensure that communication systems are in order, and disaster management drills are carried out periodically; and

(xxix) perform such other functions as the State Government or State Authority may assign to it or as it deems necessary for disaster management in the District.

(iv) Local Authorities

Functions of the local authority:

(1) Subject to the directions of the District Authority, a local authority shall—

(a) ensure that its officers and employees are trained for disaster management;

(b) ensure that resources relating to disaster management are so maintained as to be readily available for use in the event of any threatening disaster situation or disaster;

(c) ensure all construction projects under it or within its jurisdiction conform to the standards and specifications laid down for prevention of disasters and mitigation by the National Authority, State Authority and the District Authority; and

(d) carry out relief, rehabilitation and reconstruction activities in the affected area in accordance with the State Plan and the District Plan.

(2) The local authority may take such other measures as may be necessary for the disaster management.

Annual Report

(1) The National Authority shall prepare once every year, in such form and at such time as may be prescribed, an annual report giving a true and full account of its activities during the previous year and copies thereof shall be forwarded to the Central Government and that Government shall cause the same to be laid before both Houses of Parliament within one month of its receipt.

(2) The State Authority shall prepare once in every year, in such form and at such time as may be prescribed, an annual report giving a true and full account of its activities during the previous year and copies thereof shall be forwarded to the State Government and that Government shall cause the same to be laid before each House of the State Legislature where it consists of two Houses, or where such Legislature consists of one House, before that House.

INCIDENT COMMAND SYSTEM (ICS) (See Chart 3.2)

Incident Command System (ICS) was developed in early 1970s in the United States in response to a series of major wild land fires in southern California. As a response, several agencies collaborated to form the (FIRESCOPE) Firefighting Resources of California Organized for Potential Emergencies to address these difficulties and this inter-agency effort resulted in the development of ICS model of management.

The incident Command System (ICS) is an on-scene, all-risk, flexible modular system adaptable to any scale of natural as well as man-made emergency/incidents. The ICS seeks to strengthen the existing disaster response management system by ensuring that the designated controlling/responsible authorities at different levels are backed by trained incident Command Teams (ICTs), whose members have been trained in the different facets of emergency/disaster response management. The ICS will not put in place any new hierarchy or supplant the existing system, but will only reinforce it. The Members of the ICT will be jointly trained for development as a team. When an ICT is deployed for an incident, all concerned agencies of the Government will respond as per the assessment of the Team. This system therefore enables proper co-ordination amongst the different agencies of the Government. The five Command functions in the Incident Command System are as follows[2]: (See Chart 3.3)

ICS is a good strategy for disaster management which depends upon good administrative system in the country. Since government resources are always under pressure

FIGURE 3.2

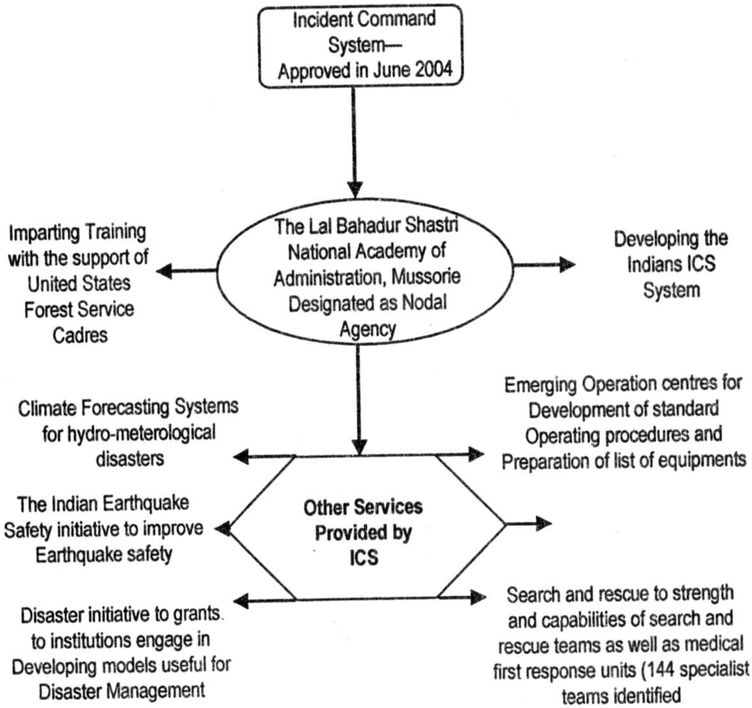

Incident Command System—Approved in June 2004
The Lal Bahadur Shastri National Academy of Administration, Mussorie Designated as Nodal Agency
Imparting Training with the support of United States Forest Service Cadres
Developing the Indians ICS System
Climate Forecasting Systems for hydro-meterological disasters
Emerging Operation centres for Development of standard Operating procedures and Preparation of list of equipments
The Indian Earthquake Safety initiative to improve Earthquake safety
Other Services Provided by ICS
Disaster initiative to grants to institutions engage in Developing models useful for Disaster Management
Search and rescue to strength and capabilities of search and rescue teams as well as medical first response units (144 specialist teams identified

FIGURE 3.3

Financial Administration
Command
Incident Command System
Mainly a Management Functions having Five Management Activities
Operations
Planning
Logistics

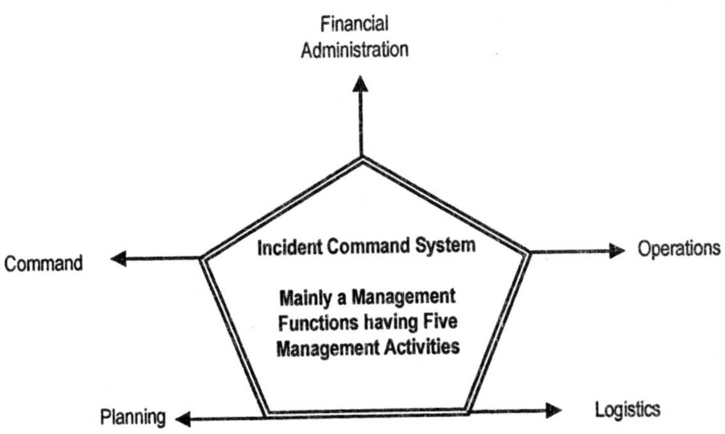

(demand exceeds supply) and expectations exceed what can be afforded), there is an on going requirement to review activities to ensure that resources are used to best effect and that government can demonstrate sound stewardship. Consequently, the point of entry for programmes to improve efficiency is commonly a requirement to reduce operating costs as part of budgetary restraint.[3] (See Chart 3.4)

CHART 3.4

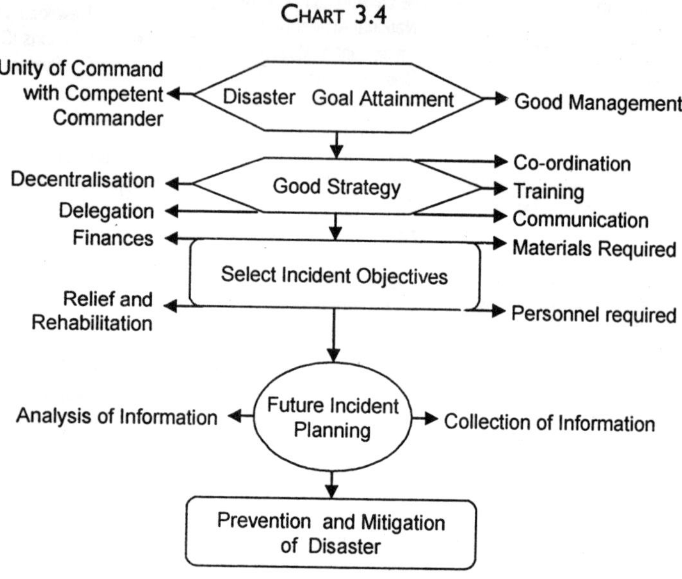

CRITICAL APPRAISAL

The infrastructural framework created to cope with disaster management as mentioned above after the enactment of Disaster Management Act, 2005 is excellent. However, whenever, any disaster takes place, the infrastructure fails to respond. Let us discuss the facts and suggestions to ensure results.

- Lack of effective, efficient and responsive Organizational set-up;
- Lack of System and transparency;

- Aapathy on the part of the political elite and top Bureaucracy to solve the problems of affected people;
- Lack of Effective leadership and communication to deal with disasters issues;
- Lack of action in right earnest: Mere paper planning to impress the press and people;
- No sincere efforts and attention to post-recovery of victims (Rehabilitation);
- Lack of reliable and quality Data; and
- Lack of community awareness.

Our vision 2020 is to build a safer and secure India through sustained collective effort, synergy of national capacities and people's participation. What looks a dream today will be transformed into reality in the next two decades. This is our goal and we shall strive to achieve this goal with a missionary zeal. The path ahead, which looks difficult today, will become a lot easier as we move along together.

Inspite of this understanding our organizational framework in India has not been effective to deal promptly with disasters. Hari Jai Singh states in his article, "Faulty System and Poor Response: Technology as a Tool For Disaster Management" in the *Daily Tribune* (Feb. 9, 2001) that despite numerous natural calamities in the past, a viable disaster management system is missing. There is no point in boasting about our information technology revolution. We have hardly used its power for the service of the people. It needs to be realized that information technology has made today's statecraft and politico-economic management virtually outdated. It is, therefore, necessary to shed the old mindset. It is not the people but the system, the persons at the helm and the poor standard of governance which have invariably failed the nation. This has once again been proved by the way of the people, here and abroad, have responded to one of the biggest disasters ever to hit the country in the wake of the devastating earthquake in Gujarat.

Amit Sengupta in his article "Dumbstruck by Devastation", in Hindustan Times *(February 8, 2001) painfully remarks that: While the bureaucracy in Bhuj and Gandhinagar and let us not forget New Delhi-twiddles its thumbs, making false claims and utterly hollow promises, reality tells a dark tale of a democracy where the political class has proved its cold insensitivity and professional inefficiency even in the face of such a disaster. There is a lesson for the people of India after this catastrophe: the hallucinatory patriotic euphoria of India being a nuclear power and a potential superpower in the new millennium is a lot of hogwash. When it comes to the mighty Indian State, it is nothing but a clueless paper tiger, a dumb, monolith. It is nowhere in sight when it comes to coping with mass tragedy as we now see in the dead cities and villages of Kutch.*

There will always be damage, deaths, grief and terror. That no one can prevent. But it can be minimized, to the extent that an effective government can, with a system that responds quickly, has access to what is needed, gets it there, mobilizes personnel and—very importantly—makes as much information available as possible

CONCLUSION

There is a Need of Transparency, Good Governance, accountability and responsiveness. It has been reported in the press. T.V. and other platforms that disaster management programmes become heaven for unscrupulous people. Money is collected and used for personal purpose. Therefore, there is a need for good account keeping, good governance and responsive administration to keep rogues out of this noble cause. Only the people with faith in ethics hardwork, sincerity, loyalty and spirit of service should be employed. A.S. Arya in his article, Action for Earth Quake Disaster Mitigation rightly suggests the following steps to be followed to provide relief:

- Quick administrative response from Centre and State levels.
- Visit of Prime Minister and Cabinet Ministers to support relief efforts.
- Immediate deployment of Defence and Para-Military forces.

- Spontaneous public response with overwhelming generosity in terms of relief assistance.
- Rapid transportation of Relief materials, food items, medical supplies/equipments.
- Liberal assistance be announced by the PM, besides financial aid from many government and non-governmental organizations.
- Overwhelming international response with personnel and material resources.

Notes and References

1 See Chart 3.1 and 3.2 for structure and Mechanism of Disaster Management at all levels.

2 GOI, Ministry of Home Affairs, LBSNAA, Source Book on "District Disaster Management", p. 85.

3 Mohan Kaul, Civil Service Reforms, Learning From Commonwealth Experience, in *IJPA*, July-Sept. 1998, p. 686.

4

Preparedness, Prevention, Mitigation and Rehabilitation

(See Chart 4.1)

I. PREPAREDNESS

Preparedness for disasters done meticulously implies half of the problem solved. In developing countries such as India, generally we do little preparedness and whatever is done; it is in a callous way. Preparedness requires meticulous planning as a small mistake would result in loss of large number of lives associated with other risks.

In the context of cyclone Dr. Mazhar Ali Sabri, in his article, "Cyclones and Disaster Management" in *Kurukshetra,* May 2000, states that Disaster preparedness is the management planning for a prompt and efficient action at all levels to save lives, to reduce suffering and to minimize damage to property when a natural disaster occurs. A comprehensive effort for disaster preparedness include public education about cyclones, awareness campaigns, provisions for issuing early cyclone, warning, organization of people, disaster training, preparing evacuation plans and providing evacuees with emergency food, water and shelter. Such an effort may be helpful in reducing the loss of life due to natural calamities. Participation of the cyclone

CHART 4.1

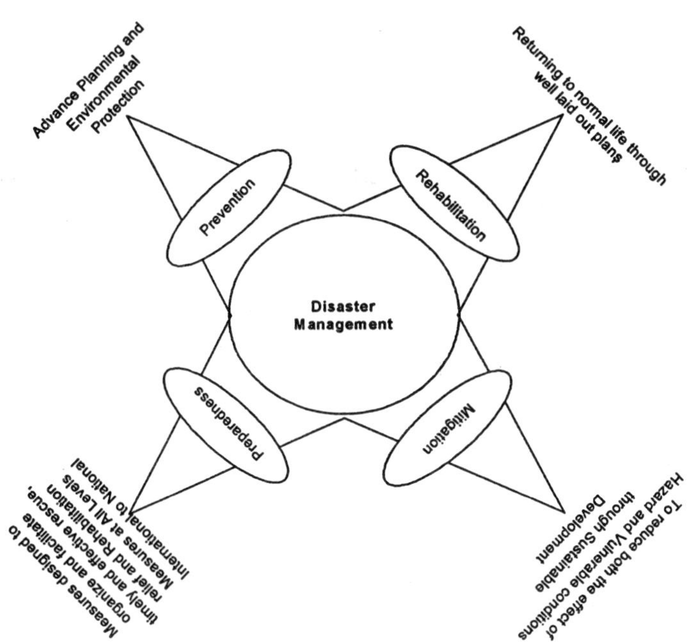

warning, organization of people, disaster training, preparing evacuation plans and providing evacuees with emergency food, water and shelter. Such an effort may be helpful in reducing the loss of life due to natural calamities. Participation of the cyclone victims is also very important as without their cooperation all outside initiatives will be just in vain. Experiences of the community should be utilized and aired in public meetings and discussions so that they can be better informed and prepared.

The objective of disaster preparedness is to ensure that responsive administration, procedures, and human, material and financial resources, available to provide quick assistance to disaster prone victims, thus promoting relief and rehabilitation services to meet their needs.

Disaster preparedness is a continuous process and forms an integral part of the national system responsible for developing plans and programs for disaster management (prevention, mitigation, preparedness, response, rehabilitation, or reconstruction). It involves the following steps:

- Identify areas or region prone to disasters;
- Establish communication, information, and warning systems;
- Design coordination and response mechanisms;
- Plan for financial and other resources for increased readiness which can be mobilized in disaster situations;
- Prepare public education programs;
- Keep the persons involved alert;
- Do not allow slackness in the system; and
- System should be ready to respond without any delay as a minute delay can cause more loss of life and property.

Those countries who prepare for containing the impact of Disaster suffer less and their normal life is restored fast while those countries where there is no preparedness suffer a lot for a long time. Hence, preparedness is the first essential step for any disaster management.

Earthquakes and other disasters are a phenomenon which cannot be stopped altogether but advance planning can mitigate sufferings what precautions are necessary is a difficult question which need research, analysis and documentation? We must initiate action on it to avoid miseries and sorrows which can be prevented. *Indian Express* Editorial (January 29, 2001) rightly suggests that the Republic Day earthquake does raise numerous questions about the quality of the country's development and disaster preparedness, about the nature of the urban planning, about the character of its housing construction, question that don't have easy answers. For the moment, however, there is no getting away from the fact that earthquakes will continue to be part of our lives, perched as we are on a vast land plate floating on an ocean of molten rock. According to informed estimates, 57 percent of the country is prone to earthquakes. The tremors of the earthquake were felt as far, away as Tamil

Nadu and Delhi. Incidentally, Kutch was hit by an earthquake in 1819 and the Sindree fort that once guarded its coastline that had collapsed under its assault. Yet, we seem to have learnt almost nothing from the past. While it is true that earthquakes cannot be predicted, the fact remains that while the 1993 Latur earthquake left over 10,000 dead, the one that had visited Los Angeles some 22 years earlier was far more severe but killed 55. One of the reasons for the heavy death tolls in India is its high population density. But it is also true that the country has not internalized any of the lessons it has learnt. from counters with death on a mass scale.

Chistiane Viedna in his article, "Disaster Alert" in *World Health,* June 1978 clearly defines that the very nature of a disaster has become more complex, since its gravity is no longer measured simply by the number of deaths but by the size of the population affected and the economic losses that result from a major upheaval in the normal pattern of life.

What do we mean by a disaster? There is no simple answer. First of all a natural phenomenon can be merely an impressive event in one region and a fearful catastrophe in another. Cyclones of comparable violence will not have the same effect if they hit Florida as they would if they hit the Bay of Bengal. In the first case, no lives at all may be lost and the material damage will be quite quickly repaired, since the United States is wealthy enough to cope. In the second case, whole houses will be carried away, cultivated field will be flooded and the crops totally lost. The inhabitants of Florida will have got away with a fright; those of the Bay of Bengal will be rendered homeless, threatened by famine, disease and the loss of livelihood. These differences clearly suggests that USA has done a hard work for advance preparedness for disaster mitigation while in India, we either did not prepare or prepared only on paper. In India, preparedness is only a theoretical exercise.

The United Nations Disaster Relief Office (UNDRO) defines Disaster Preparedness as "(a series of) measures designed to organize and facilitate timely and effective rescue, relief and rehabilitation operations in cases of disaster. Measures of preparedness include among others, setting up disaster relief machinery, formulation of emergency relief plans, training of specific groups (and vulnerable communities) to undertake rescue and relief, stock piling supplies and earmarking funds for relief operations".

This protective process embraces measures which enable governments, communities and individuals to respond rapidly to disaster situations to cope with them effectively. Preparedness includes the formulation of viable emergency plans, the development of warning systems, the maintenance of inventories and the training of personnel. It may also embrace search and rescue measures as well as evacuation plans for areas that may be at risk from a recurring disaster.

Preparedness therefore encompasses those measures taken before a disaster event which are aimed at minimizing loss of life, disruption of critical services, and damage when the disaster occurs. All preparedness planning needs to be supported by appropriate legislation with clear allocation of responsibilities and budgetary provisions.

Any preparedness strategy has to aim at:

- Developing awareness amongst the people to be alert and responsive to impending disasters.
- Reducing the vulnerability of community in disaster-prone areas and enhancing their ability to cope with them.
- Strenghtening the institutional mechanisms and capacities of government at several levels, non-governmental organizations (NGOs) and communities in disaster preparedness, relief, response and rehabilitation activities.
- Building networks between several organizations including government, NGOs, private organizations, community, and other key stakeholders to foster preparedness efforts.

An disaster preparedness programme needs to include certain important principles. Some of these according to Alley (1993) are:

- Perceptions should be studied and opportunities created for people to modify their perceptions where necessary.

- Create strategies to rouse the curiosity of the individual and encourage a general desire for change.
- Individual and communities should be helped to compare the existing ways with proposed innovations, relate innovations to the basic needs and overcome barriers to acceptance.
- Adopt educational methods that have a heavy emphasis on community involvement and participation.
- Learning by doing and developing participation in various activities related to identification of disaster preparedness needs.
- Groups approval influences adoption of new behaviour patterns. In traditional societies, most of the decisions regarding new practices are multi-personal decisions, the role of the family and other social groups being the determining factors.
- Behaviour is motivated. Motivation is the inner drive that propels all human beings to move towards attaining a desired goal.
- Disaster preparedness behaviour is concerned with changes in knowledge, attitude and behaviour and the ultimate goal is sustained for disaster preparedness behaviour.
- Since different agencies work simultanesouly at the community level, it is necessary for them to come to an understanding in order to avoid the dissemination of conflicting advice.
- Psychological factors are not the only determinants in behaviour. They combine and interact with physical, social and other factors.

Preparedness involves several activities such as:

- Developing and institutionalizing disaster preparedness plan which is comprehensive, indicating the roles and responsibilities of several stakeholders before, during and after the occurrence of disasters.

- Strengthening warning systems and meterological studies.
- Evolving appropriate information, education and communication (IEC) activities for community.
- Keeping ready Rapid Response Teams, search and Rescue personnel alongwith Emergency Medical Teams.
- Setting up safe havens.
- Putting in place emergency evacuation procedures.
- Making available relief activities including emergency shelters, medical, foods, first aid services, and security arrangements.
- Assessing the damage after the occurrence and restoring transport, power, and communication systems.

PREVENTION

A culture of prevention, it was felt needs to be installed in all communities and amongst disaster managers. This requires active involvement of all groups of society, national, international organisations, governments and private organisations. Early warnings and conscious developmental planning are the key elements of preventive planning. The new culture that is permeating the disaster management in the present times is based on the premise that hazards both natural and human-induced are inevitable, but the disasters that follow can be handled effectively through adequate preventive measures.

Principles of Disaster Prevention

- Risk assessment is a required step for the adoption of adequate and successful disaster reduction policies.
- Disaster prevention and preparedness are of primary importance in reducing the need for disaster relief.
- Disaster prevention and preparedness should be considered an integral part of the developmental

policy and planning at the national, regional, bilateral, multilateral and international levels.

- Early warning of impending disasters and their effective dissemination using telecommunication are the key factors to successful prevention and preparedness.
- Prevention measures are most effective when they involve participation at all levels, from the local, community, national to the regional and international levels.
- Vulnerability can be reduced by the application of proper design and patterns of development focused on target groups through appropriate education and training.
- The international community accepts the need to share necessary technology to prevent, reduce and mitigate disasters which should be made freely available and done in a timely manner as an integral part of technical cooperation.
- Each country bears the primary responsibility of protecting its people, infrastructure and other national assets from the impact of natural disasters. The international community should demonstrate strong political determination required to mobilise and make efficient use of existing resources, including financial, scientific and technological means (High Powered Committee Report, 2001).

Disaster Prevention requires various measures which any country needs to adopt. This includes:

1. Integrating disaster prevention with national development plans. The culture of disaster prevention needs to be a part of development plans and projects. Measures directed at reducing the occurrence of floods through construction of embankments, etc. promoting earthquake resistant structures, watershed management, rainwater harvesting, alternative cropping patterns, etc. to

manage situations of drought are efforts towards disaster prevention.

2. Formulating a disaster management policy for the whole country, providing for a legal framework for the management of all types of disasters in a comprehensive manner. This facilitates the proper implementation of preventive measures at all levels by the concerned organisations.
3. Making the community aware, educated and their capacities built to manage disasters. A community leadership is to be built, to make them self-reliant and resilient to cope with disasters.
4. Involving educational, training institutions, corporate sectors, and non-governmental organisations (NGOs) in eliciting public participation, generating awareness among all concerned stakeholders.
5. Strengthening of existing infrastructure such as buildings, communication system, water supply, sanitation facilities, etc.

MITIGATION

Mitigation embraces all measures taken to reduce both the effect of the hazard itself and the vulnerable conditions to it in order to reduce the scale of a future disaster. Therefore, mitigation activities can be focused on the hazard itself or the elements exposed to the threat. Examples of mitigation measures which are hazard specific include modifying the occurrence of the hazard, e.g. water management in drought prone areas, avoiding the hazard by sitting people away from the hazard and by strengthening structures to reduce damage when a hazard occurs. In addition to these physical measures, mitigation should also be aimed at reducing the physical, economic and social vulnerability to threats and the underlying causes for this vulnerability.

There is no centralised comprehensive policy or programme of Government of India regarding disaster mitigation. But the government acts as the biggest insurer to 'help the population in distress due to any natural calamity through relief and rehabilitation programmes. loans and subsidies. At this stage, a number of voluntary agencies also come forward in a big way to help mitigate the disastrous effects on the population. Contingency plans are normally available with the district administration and civil defence authorities for use after every minor or major disaster. However, a number of government departments and institutions are engaged in activities, which are multifaceted in nature. It is a team effort.

The Tenth Five Year Plan states that sustainability is the key word in the development process. Development activities that do not consider the disaster loss perspective fail to be sustainable. The compounded costs of disasters relating to loss of life, assets, economic activities, and cost of reconstruction of not only assets but of lives can scarcely be borne by any community or nation. Therefore, all development schemes in vulnerable areas should include disaster mitigation analysis, whereby the feasibility of a project is assessed with respect to vulnerability of the area and the mitigation measures required for sustainability. Environmental protection, afforestation programmes, pollution control, construction of earthquake-resistant structures, etc. should therefore be given high priority in the plans.

The significance of mitigation arises from the fact that any effort in preempting the occurrence of disaster, saves resources be it personnel, finance, physical assets, etc. The huge amount of financial resources allocated to mitigation activities reduces the demand for money towards emergency recovery, repair and reconstruction. Mitigation, since it aims at prevention and preparedness, ensures socio-economic continuity, sustainability and socio-environmental health of the community.

P.D. Amarasinghe, Sri Lanka's Secretary in the Ministry of Disaster Management and Human Rights stressed the importance of a comprehensive risk mitigation and prevention strategy if countries' national development goals or the Millennium Development Goals are to be met.

Abravovtiz Living with Risk, taken from A global review of disaster reduction initiatives, ISDR, 2004 states that while we cannot do way with natural hazards, we can eliminate those we cause, minimize those we exacerbate, and reduce our vulnerability to most. Doing this requires healthy and resilient communities and ecosystems. Viewed in this light, disaster mitigation is clearly part of a broader strategy of sustainable development- making communities and nations socially, economically and ecologically sustainable.

Increasingly, countries have come to realize that the development activity and disaster risk reduction are two sides of the same coin and have, therefore, to be dealt with in unison. Mainstreaming disaster risk management into development policy, planning and implementation has thus become an important agenda for many countries. The Asian Disaster Preparedness Centre (ADPC) based in Bangkok, Thailand has embarked on a project for Advocacy and Capacity Buidling for Mainstreaming Disaster Risk Management in Development Practice (MDRM), aiming at promoting the mainstreaming of disaster risk management into sustainable development policies and practice throughout Asia.

We may keep the following in mind to ensure mitigation:

- Integrating disaster mitigation with development plans.
- Effective communication systems.
- Use of latest information technology.
- Insurance in all relevant sectors.
- Extensive public awareness and education campaigns particularly in rural areas.
- Legal and legislative support.
- Greater involvement of NGOs/private sector; and
- Allocating separate money for disaster relief in normal budget; and a strict review of housing, drainage, etc. to ensure long range solutions to the problems.

There are certain principles of disaster mitigation. These include:

(i) Creating awareness of risk at community level.

(ii) Promoting local actions through community participation to reduce such risks.

(iii) Incorporating mitigation measures in the national and regional development plans, land-use planning proposals and in project design and appraisal in hazard-prone areas.

(iv) Assisting decision-makers (politicians and administration) to understand the nature and extent of various risks faced by communities, and assessing the economic effects of natural disasters on agricultural, commerce and industry.

(v) Demonstrating ways and means to reduce those risks within the limits of national, regional or socio-economic conditions through proper decision-making and planning.

(vi) Introducing effective measures to implement disaster mitigation plans at the different levels of government based on risk assessment and vulnerability analysis.

There are two approaches of mitigation—Structured and Non-structured.

Structural approach for mitigation may refer to both:

(a) Engineered Structures; and

(b) Non-engineered Structures.

Engineered structures involve architects and engineers during the planning, designing and construction of structures, including buildings, dams, embankments, roads, bridges, etc. Many countries have rules and laws providing codes for engineered construction. These codes provide guidelines for appropriate design and construction techniques in disaster prone areas for specific disasters such as earthquakes and cyclones. Such structures can be constructed after collecting data for hazard vulnerability and related meteorological parameters (wind velocity, direction, rainfall, its duration, etc.). Structural measures include construction of cyclone shelters, coastal embankments that help protect coastal land from inundation by tidal waves and storm surges, water harvesting facilities, etc.

Non-engineered structures are generally constructed by people with the help of local artisans like masons, carpenters, etc. using locally available raw material. These structures can be made safer, if people are trained and given improved designs. These structures are normally of low-cost but have less strength/resistance for a disaster.

Non-structural Approach

Non-structural approach encompasses those measures that attempt to bring about coordination of efforts between all organisations and persons during all phases of disaster management, training and public awareness, legislation, policy-making, preparing of action plans, etc. Such approach to mitigation consists of positive actions through legislation, incentives, educating people, creating community awareness, etc.

Disaster Mitigation is a complex, process and a challenging task. Structural infrastructure helps a lot in mitigation but is not sufficient to meet all the requirements of disaster-affected population/area. There is a need also for non-structured approach which is flexible, innovative and even dedicated to meeting the needs of disaster-affected people/area. We can thus conclude that both structured and non-structured measures supplement each other, i.e. both are indispensable.

REHABILITATION (See Chart 4.2)

Rehabilitation is essential to integrate the disaster affected people in normal community life through Government, NGOs and Community participation

There is no doubt that hazards are integral aspects of our environment. Disaster management is normally viewed as a post-disaster mitigation focusing on rescue, relief and rehabilitation in the events such as earthquakes, cyclones, floods, droughts and fires. It has been realized that effect of disasters on human population can be mitigated, if not averted altogether, by integrating disaster prevention and mitigation with development planning.

CHART 4.2

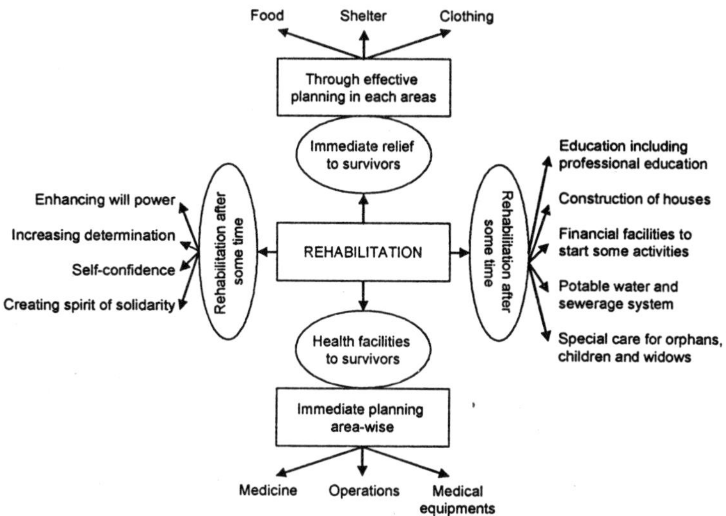

Ingredients of Effective Rehabilitation

1. Need of Preparing disaster plan area-wise.
2. Effective co-ordination to avoid delays and provide timely helps.
3. Psychological counseling to kindle will power among the disaster affected people.
4. Harmony and goodwill among all sections of the society and not party politics, communalism or regionalism is the need of the hour.
5. Need of good government through dedicated, honest and hardworking personnel in administration.
6. Creating confidence, will power and self-determination among the people.
7. Involvement of NGO's should be utilized in social welfare especially women and child welfare.
8. Construction of houses should be as per the need of the people and area and not be made under the influence of builders for consideration.

9. Need of effective leadership at all levels.
10. Designing proper management information system (MIS) for disaster management.
11. Need of Enacting safety laws in time to avoid tragedies.
12. Effective and efficient administration

CONCLUSION

For relief and rehabilitation, effective and efficient administration is needed after a disaster occurs. Disaster management requires good administration and commitment by all, i.e. Government, people, and voluntary organizations. The capacity and capability must be built to handle post-earthquake effects. Training programmes are essential. Duplication of efforts should be minimized and financial resources appropriately controlled to ensure transparency and best results. Governments cannot rely on normal processes to implement appropriate responses they will need to learn special skills, techniques and attitudes in dealing with the rehabilitation of earthquake victims. We can sum up briefly the essentials of rehabilitation:

(a) Treatment and care of victims through provision of goods and services and especially sympathy.
(b) Restoration of essential services such as communications, water supply and power supply as early as possible.
(c) Information and advice to the public.
(d) Maintenance of public morale and motivation.
(e) Counselling of victims and relatives.
(f) Measures for long-term rehabilitation.
(g) Goods inventory management.
(h) Monitoring at regular intervals.
(i) Allocation of duties and responsibilities clearly to avoid ambiguity.
(j) Provision of shelters for human beings and animals.
(k) People's participation in their own welfare.

Carl Sagan in his magnificent, awe inspiring work Cosmos has described human predicament and dilemmas that surround us in the most thought-provoking manner:

> "The earth is a lovely and more or less placid place. Things change, but slowly. We can lead a full life and never personally encounter. A natural disaster more violent than a storm. And so we become complacent, relaxed, unconcerned. But in the history of Nature, the record is clear. Worlds have been devastated. Even we humans have achieved the dubious technical distinction of being able to make our own disasters, both intentional and inadvertent. On the landscapes of other planets where the records of the past have been preserved there is abundant evidence of major catastrophes. It is all a matter of time scale. An event that would be unthinkable in a hundred years may be inevitable in a hundred million."

Our lovely blue planet, the Earth, is the only home we know. Venus is too hot. Mars is too cold. But the Earth is just right, a heaven for humans. After all, we evolved here. But our congenial climate may be unstable. We are perturbing our poor planet in serious and contradictory ways. Is there any danger of driving the environment of the earth towards the planetary Hell of Venus or the global ice age of Mars? The simple answer is that nobody knows. The study of the global climate, the comparison of the Earth with other worlds, are subjects in their earliest stages of development. They are fields that are poorly and grudgingly funded. In our ignorance, we continue to push and pull, to pollute the atmosphere and brighten the land, oblivious of the fact that the long-term consequences are largely unknown.

A few million years ago, when human beings first evolved on Earth, it was already a middle aged world, 4.6 billion years long from the catastrophes and impetuosities of its youth. But we humans now represent and perhaps decisions factor. Our intelligence and our technology have given us the power to affect the climate. How will we use this power? Are we willing to tolerate ignorance and complacency in matters that affect the entire human family? Do we value short-term advantages above the welfare of the Earth? Or will we think on longer time scales, with concern for our children and our grandchildren, to understand and protect the complex life-support system of our planet? The Earth is a tiny and fragile world. It needs to be cherished.

5

Effective and Efficient Public Administration for Disaster Administration

Planning itself will be of no use until and unless we have an efficient administration system based on good governance especially to tackle disaster related issues. It has been seen in all disasters whether earthquake, drought, cyclone or even a small accident, our administrative system goes out of gear and people are left at their own mercy with hit and trial approach. Disaster preparedness requires that public administration must be prompt and responsive and not tied to red tapism. (See Chart 5.1)

According to E.N. Gladden, administration means ".... to care for, or look after people, to manage affairs is determined action taken in pursuit of common purpose."[1] Nigro observes, "Administration is the organization and use of men and materials to accomplish a purpose" Public Administration:

(i) is cooperative group effort in a public setting;

(ii) covers all the branches—executive, legislative and judicial—and their inter-relationships.

(iii) has an important role in the formulation of public policy and is thus a part of the political process;

CHART 5.1

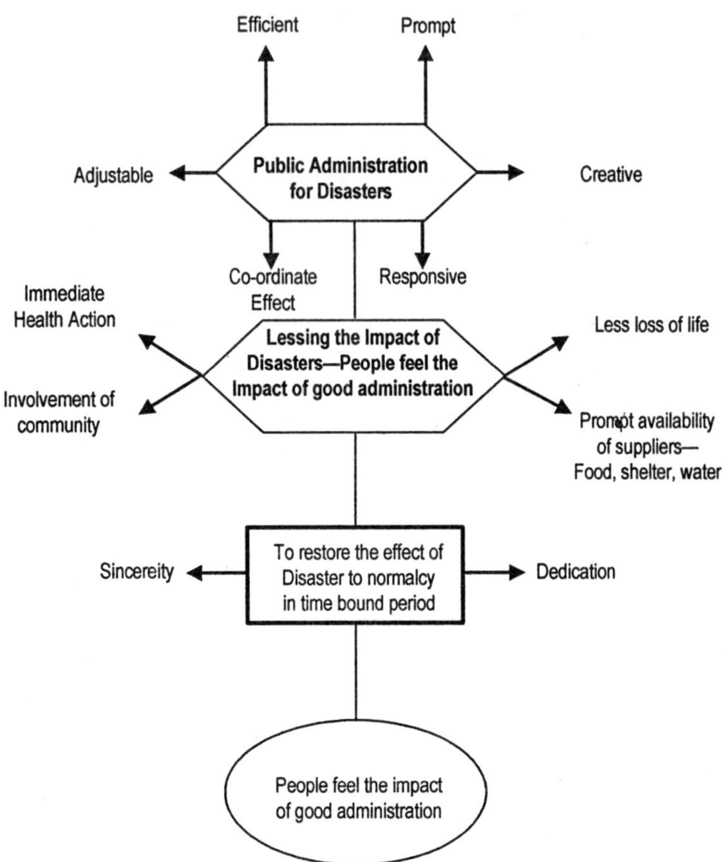

(iv) Is more important than, and also different in significant ways from private administration;

(v) As a field of study and practice has been much influenced in recent years by the human relations approach; and

(vi) Is closely associated with numerous private groups and individuals in providing services to the community.[2]

To White, "the art of administration is the direction, co-ordination and control of many persons to achieve some purpose or objective of Public Administration and consists of all those operations having for their purpose the fulfillment or enforcement of public policy.[3]

According to F.M. Marx, administration is determined action taken in pursuit of a conscious purpose. It is the systematic order of the affairs and the calculated use of resources, aimed at making those things happen which one wants to happen and forestalling everything to the contrary.

In the words of the Woodrow Wilson, "Public administration is detailed and systematic application of law. Every application of law is an act of administration.[4]

According to Pfiffner, "Public administration consists of doing the work of the Government, whether it is be running an X-Ray machine in a health laboratory or coining money in the mint.... Administration consists of getting the work of government done by co-ordinating the efforts of people so that they can work together or accomplish their set tasks. Administration embraces activities which may be highly "technical and specialized, as public health and the building of bridges... It also involves managing, directing, and supervising the activities of thousands, even millions of workers so that some order and efficiency may result from their efforts."[5]

COMPONENTS OF PUBLIC ADMINISTRATION (Chart 5.2)

An analysis of the definitions of public administration would throw light on the qualities of good administration. We may sum up, briefly, the components of good public administration:

(a) helps in formulation of policies (political, economic, social, industrial, which are realistic, feasible and practical,

(b) helps in formulating of long-term and short-term plans aimed at harnessing the potential resources,

(c) supports execution of policies and plans,

CHART 5.2

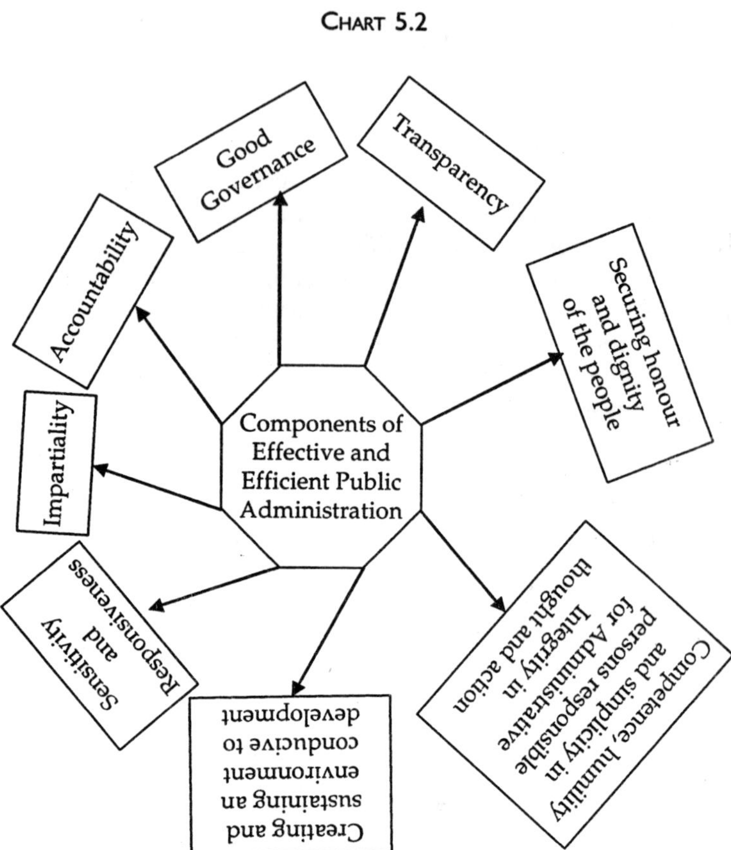

(d) keeps the administrative system in tune with the needs of the country through administrative improvements and reforms,
(e) helps in resource mobilisation and utilisation,
(f) develops supportive linkages with political elite, people, and foreign countries to ensure political development, people's participation and good international relations, and
(g) develops responsibility in administration.

Mr. M.G. Devashayam, an ex-IAS officer, in his Article, 'Good Administration' in the *Daily Tribune* mentions the components of responsible administration. These are:

(i) Openness in the sense of having wide contact with the people administered;

(ii) A sense of justice, fair play and impartiality in dealing with men and matters;

(iii) Sensitivity and responsiveness to the urges, feelings and aspirations of the common people;

(iv) Securing the honour and dignity of the human being, however humble he or she might be;

(v) Humility and simplicity in the persons manning the administrative machinery and their easy accessibility;

(vi) Creating and sustaining an atmosphere conducive to development, growth and social change; and

(vii) Honesty and integrity in thought and action.

Mr. Harish Khare in his article, 'Role for Bureaucracy; Soft State Soft Administrators' in *The Times of India* dated 2 February, 1993, urges the bureaucracy to exert for the development of the country in the face of failing political leadership. To quote him, "The Bureaucracy thus will have to explore the extent of its own constitutional leeway in order to ensure that the best interests of the Republic are not mortgaged by an irresponsible and shortsighted political class. Man for Man, the bureaucrats can certainly have the better of the politicians without in anyway transgressing constitutional obligations or administrative norms."[6]

ESSENTIALS OF DISASTER ADMINISTRATION

(i) Need of Effective Public Administration for Disaster Administration

Public Administration is the heart of development. Any systematic effort towards disaster administration must be preceded by, or coupled with efforts, to make more effective the functioning of governmental machinery. Disaster administration is essential both for developed and developing countries. All types of disasters can be tackled with a good system of disaster administration.

(ii) Meticulous Preparedness by Streamlining Administration

Public Administration has to ensure planning and implementation of disasters of all types of administration. So public administration has to ensure prevention, preparedness, rescue, relief and rehabilitation of the people affected by disasters. No attention was paid to administration of earthquake in Gujarat resulting into loss of thousands of lives.

Bhaskar Ghose in his article in the context of Gujarat earthquake, "The Final Countdown" in *The Hindustan Time* dated Feb. 8, 2001 suggests that we cannot stop such disasters. What is needed is to learn from failures and make the administrative system perfect for future to take care of all mistakes and faults in advance. He has pointed out that we will continue to live in the shadow of peril, and we will never know when it will come, whether it will come at all, and if it does, what shape it will take. But life must continue; shops must open and do business, offices must engage in whatever activity they are there to do, trains must run, power units function (in the manner in which they're used to). In short, it has to be business as usual. Even in Gujarat, when the dead have been cremated or buried, when they have come to some kind of terms with grief and devastation, the business of living will continue. What we would call everyday living will, of necessity, be resumed, as time passes.

(iii) Prompt and Effective Administration for Effective Preparedness

It is time for a system to be put in place which, firstly and most importantly, is under the direct control of one person, is capable of quick ordered reaction to a calamity, has access to information on the location of material and equipment, is able to mobilise personnel, and which is, by law, the overriding authority in a crisis, with the legal backing to issue instructions to all agencies of Government, civic bodies, and of private agencies which have to be carried out immediately. Its relations with the armed forces will need to be worked out in clear, unambiguous terms.

Disasters will occur; we don't need astrologers pouring over their grubby rolls of papers and manuals to tell us that.

We have to live with them and carry on living. As someone said, it is be now, 'tis not to come; if it be not to come, it will be now; if it be not now, yet it will come: the readiness is all important.

Amit Sengupta in his article, "Dumbstruck by Devastation" in *Hindustan Times* (Feb. 8, 2001) painfully remarks that: While the bureaucracy in Bhuj and Gandhinagar—and let us not forget New Delhi—twiddles its thumbs, making false claims and utterly hollow promises, reality tells a dark tale of a democracy where the political class has proved its cold insensitivity and, professional inefficiency even in the face of such a disaster. There is a lesson for the people of India after this catastrophe: the hallucinatory patriotic euphoria of India being a nuclear power and a potential superpower in the new millennium is a lot of hogwash. When it comes to the mighty Indian State, it is nothing but a clueless paper tiger, a dumb, monolith. It is nowhere in sight when it comes to coping with mass tragedy as we now see in the dead cities and villages of Kutch.

For citizens, in this ravaged society, the Government does not exist. These comments by those who have actually seen the events happening cause pain and agony in everybody's mind and raises many questions. What have we achieved after more than 50 years of independence? Our own elected government is making a fool of the people. They have different priorities except the people who are suffering in misery in this dark time of their life.

There will always be damage, deaths, grief and terror. That no one can prevent. But it can be minimized, to the extent that an effective government can, with a system that responds quickly, has access to what is needed, gets it there, mobilizes personnel and — very importantly makes as much information available as possible

IV. COOPERATION AND PARTICIPATION OF PEOPLE

Administration is never something apart from people and their needs; rather it is the means by which these needs are met and the administrator who thinks of his organization as something apart from the community will fail to recognize significant problems of the citizens and the administration will not be in a position to deliver the goods.

ARC has also observed in this very connection: "If, in the prosperity of the people, lies the strength of a government, it is in their contentment that lies the security and stability of democracy."

V. CONCERN FOR PEOPLE

However in Gujarat, during earthquake and after that, we find that Politico-administrative leadership never realized their obligations to the people. They remained dumb spectators worrying only of their family and near and dear ones. They forgot their duties. Let us mention the comments of some eminent persons.

Inder Malhotra is very critical of Indian bureaucracy and Political Elite in handling Gujarat Earthquake situation. In his article, "Nightmare of Gujarat's Mega-quake" in *The Tribune* dated February 1, 2001 he clearly stated that Official media informed the country, in a tone that had a touch of crowing about it, that the Cabinet Crisis Management Committee (CMC)—consisting of top bureaucrats and technocrats—at 3 p.m. Instead of being pleased about it, all concerned ought to be ashamed. The worthy members of the committee ought to have quietly left the parade and buckled down to their primary responsibility without losing a single second. The deplorable delay on their part only underscores that no lessons were learnt from the similar dithering at the time of the hijacking of the IC-814 13 months ago.

VI. PROMPT AND FAST

Then also it had taken several hours for the Cabinet Crisis Committees to assemble. To compound this failing official spokes persons trotted out the excuse that it took time to inform all the members of the committee who were busy in various parts of the city. In heaven's name what are the cellular phones that the taxpayer provides to every official above a certain rank meant for? Indeed, why should it be necessary to summon the CMC members at all? At the first hint of a major crisis like the one that has overtaken the country they must automatically head for the pre-arranged spot, usually the Cabinet Secretary's office. This happens, as a matter of course, in all countries where governance hasn't deteriorated to the extent it has here. Reaction time in New Delhi to the super-cyclone in Orissa was equally long. It chills the blood to contemplate what might happen if there is similar lackadaisical approach to, God forbid, a nuclear threat to this country.

Bureaucratic file push of shaking earth and souls in slum being cannot be permitted to become a substitute for work on the ground. Above all, no one should forget that the Oriya victims of the cyclone and even the sufferers from Bhopal gas tragedy of 1984 have not yet been fully compensated or rehabilitated. This shameful history must not be allowed to repeat itself now or ever again. Even the same paper editorial was very critical. To quote: "The first who should be rapped on the knuckles are the members of the Central Crisis Management Committee, comprising top bureaucrats, who got together at 3 p.m. for discussing the calamity which befall Gujarat minutes before the President arrived at Rajpath for taking the salute at the Republic Day Parade. It is a matter of great shame even for central leadership who continued enjoying the Republic Day and did not bother to take stock of the Gujarat situation. Republic Day celebrations after the Gujarat News clearly prove that the Republic is for the political elite and not for the people. This has made our preamble a hollow enunciation.

(VII) DIFFERENCE BETWEEN GOOD AND POOR PUBLIC ADMINISTRATION

Let us substantiate it with some examples that how good preparedness, prevention and mitigation can lessen the impact of disaster.

Christiane Viedma in his article, "Disaster Alert", in *World Health*, June 1978 stated that the 1976 earthquake in Guatemala provided a striking example of the unequal effects of a natural phenomenon. Generally speaking, homes in the wealthy suburbs stayed up, and the householders suffered little more than the loss of a favourite vase. Homes in the poorer quarters mostly crashed down at the first shock. The result was that those people who were not killed outright lost all their possessions. Drainage channels were destroyed in some places, so that waste waters mingled with domestic water supplies and contaminated them. In the space of a few minutes, an already impoverished population found itself defenseless against the twin threat of hunger and disease.

The reasons underlying this unfair situation are obvious. The rich suburbs had been sited in the safest zones and were built of quake-proof materials. The poorest houses were often constructed by their owners' hands from adobe-bricks of dry mud—which are quite incapable of withstanding sudden shocks; they were also unplanned and therefore tended to be built in the most precarious places. People made their homes wherever a site was available reasonably close to the basic building materials—and no doubt the same sort of houses will have been rebuilt on exactly the same spot since there is nowhere else to go.

So a natural phenomenon may not be a disaster in itself, but only in the effect it has on people. Throughout the developing countries, 95 per cent of such events leave victims behind them, and all of them have dire consequences for the national economy. There is a distinct geographic correlation between disaster prone regions and the countries that are still in the process of development.

It may well be asked how a disaster can be avoided. One particularly good example comes from China. On 4 February 1975, the entire population of the town of Haicheng—some 100,000 people—were evacuated in a matter of hours before it was utterly destroyed by an extremely violent earthquake. More than one million people live in the affected area, yet the number of victims did not exceed 200. This remarkable feat came about thanks to an extremely well-organized early warning system and a highly developed civic spirit. Seismic stations had registered abnormalities, observers had noticed unusual behaviour among animals, and after an earlier false alarm the population had already been evacuated once. But the townsfolk were quite ready to repeat the exercise when danger loomed again on the morning of 4 February. Teams of volunteers took charge of helping the sick and handicapped and checked every house to make sure that nobody was left in the town. This example stands on its own, it is true, but it teaches us that prevention is genuinely possible.

How can we have from the existing administrative machinery in India at all levels to tackle disasters when even the existing minor problems of day-to-day occurrence are in a great mess.

Today India is run through traditional administration, based on outdated processes and procedures, corrupt practices, and ill-equipped politico-administrative leadership. Henderson and Dwivedi in their brilliant article, "Administered Development; the Fifth Decade, 1990's" have warned the developing countries of poor performance if they do not improve their administrative system.

To quote them: "The emergent administrative system tended to be imitative and ritualistic. Generally practices, styles and structures of administration unrelated to local traditions, needs and realities succeeded in reproducing the symbolism, but not the substance of a British, French or American bureaucracy. Administrative reforms when and if attempted, tended to have the long-run consequence of strengthening the old framework. . . . the developing nations have a vital stake in orderly functioning of their administrative systems. The time has come for them to opt for accelerated development so as to catch the progress thwarted by their creation of a thicket of rules/regulations/ permits, and the like, in past. The 1990s will test their capability if they are able to mobilize their financial and human resources. They can ill-afford another decade of stagnation or arrest of growth; and further, they should know that economic prosperity is not the monopoly of the West alone; anyone can aspire and achieve that but not by remaining a passerby."

Ideals of the welfare state progress, prosperity and protection—to the common man can be secured only through impartial, honest and efficient administration. In the words of Prof. Charles Beard, "the future of civilized government, and even I think of civilization itself, rests upon our ability to develop a science, a philosophy and practice of administration competent to discharge the functions of civilized society." Thus, there is a need that public administration must be modernized, i.e. recreated, renewed and revitalized to produce the redesigned changes and output necessary to provide goods and services to the people at the minimum cost. This needs a different trend and magnitude of administration management, culture and capability.

The administrative capability of a government and the manner in which the disaster programmes are likely to be carried out are intimately related. On the other hand, administrative inadequacies in a national government have a retarding influence on economic and social development. These deficiencies prevent the vast flood of money, talent and material from achieving their objectives as has been the case in Gujarat.

To fulfil the aspirations of the people as mentioned in the Preamble and later stressed through directive principles of State policy and fundamental rights and other constitutional provisions, an elaborative machinery of government consisting of a complex of organizations, exists at Union, State and regional and local levels and is in operation. As the felt needs of the people take concrete forms through legislation at Union/State levels administrative discretion, new infrastructure is added in the machinery of Government, like Ministry of Welfare, Rural Development, etc. to meet the growing needs of the country. Similarly, the existing structure which has become redundant is eliminated. However, in India and other developing countries, the process of removing the structures which have become useless is very slow resulting in wastage of resources for maintaining such unproductive structures. Besides, there are many duplicate structures with overlapping functions which also lead to a great wastage of resources and efforts. Procedures are laid out to define the steps according to which administration puts policies into action. "It is procedure", as Waldo says, "that governs the routine internal and external relationship between one individual and another, between one organizational unit and another; between one process and another, between one skill or technique and another; between the organization and the public, and between all combinations and permutations of these."

These procedures, in Indian administration, instead of being an asset, have created innumerable problems leading to red tapism. Procedures have taken precedence over performance. Many reforms in financial, personnel and general procedures have been introduced. Based upon ARC recommendations, Desk Officer system, functional file Index system, proper Space layout, etc. were introduced in the machinery of government. In spite of awareness and some action, administrative procedures are acting as hurdles in the process of development and modernization. A consistent and persistent attention is required to keep the procedures in turn with the administration aimed at positive action.

There is a need for locating the problems of administration which bedevil the implementation of programmes in each sector. These problems need to be analysed and examined. Besides, all the reports of administrative reforms in general and sector-wise may also be put together to locate the bottlenecks. On the basis of these findings, action needs to be taken immediately, followed by necessary follow-up to keep the machinery of administration smooth and frictionless. Disaster Administration has not an important place in the administration of Union, State and District Administration till the Disaster Management Act, 2005 was enacted.

It would be appropriate to quote the views of the Planning Commission as laid down in Eighth Five Year Plans to improve the administrative system in India—

(i) Strengthening the people's bodies at local levels, i.e. Panchayati Raj and Urban Local Bodies to tackle disasters.

(ii) Integrated area development approach by bringing about a convergence of all the sectoral agencies concerned at the micro-level to take care of disasters impact.

(iii) Involvement of beneficiaries in the implementation of the disaster programmes through organization of beneficiaries and/or panchayats.

(iv) Introducing flexibility in the programmes by giving more autonomy to the local bodies and panchayats to plan according to the needs and resources available at the local area level for disaster preparedness and prevention.

(v) Handling over the management and supervision of local disaster problems.

(vi) Greater involvement of voluntary agencies who have the ability to demonstrate and innovate, provide technology and training, and act as support mechanism to local level institutions in disaster administration.

(vii) Streamlining of organizations at various levels so that overheads are cut down, delays are reduced, necessary funds are made available to local agencies in time, various sanctions are issued and dedicated manpower and other inputs made available in time so that disaster like situations may be tackled promptly.

(viii) A concerted effort to involve and train officials as well as non-officials, not only to bring required skills for planning and implementation but also to inculcate the required attitudes and impart the necessary knowledge about the management of disasters programmes at local levels.

(ix) Devising effective system of monitoring and evaluation of disaster programmes, more in terms of ultimate benefits than of expenditure incurred or inputs used. For example, the ultimate benefit of the Disaster programme is saving of people and properly.

No administrative system to tackle disasters can ever be absolutely perfect, and in order to achieve some sort of perfection, it has to engage itself with the help of O&M cells in devising ways and means for improvement which have to be adopted in the light of a nation's basic policies and programmes. We may keep the above-mentioned factors which impede the growth of the efforts of O&M to inject the required changes in the organizations, process and philosophy of administration to lessen the impact of disasters. The ultimate success of the measures suggested by O&M cells depends, to a great extent, upon the effective implementation of the disaster prevention measures suggested. The Third Five Year Plan has rightly commented:

> "Nevertheless, without a concerted attempt to make the administration much more action-oriented than at present, these may not yield enough results."

Administrative Ethics and Development Administration are essential to help people during and after disaster. Let us discuss them.

No administration system can ever be absolutely perfect, and in order to achieve some sort of perfection, it has to engage itself with the help of O and M cells in devising ways and means for improvement which have to be adopted in the light of a nation's basic policies and programmes. We may keep the above-mentioned factors which impede the growth of the efforts of O&M to inject the required changes in the organizations, process and philosophy of administration to manage disasters. The ultimate success of the measures suggested by O&M cells depends, to a great extent, upon the effective implementation of the measures suggested. The Third Five Year Plan has rightly commented: "Nevertheless, without a concerted attempt to make the administration much more action-oriented than at present, these may not yield enough results".

CONCLUSION

Good Public administration or good governance is essential in normal times. It becomes of prime importance to take care of people during disaster through efficient and prompt disaster administration. The true test of the good governance is tested during such periods of turbulence and disasters. Even our administration has failed to tackle man-made disasters where there is great loss of life and property which a poor country like India cannot afford, what to talk of natural disaster. Violence in the country has become a daily phenomenon. Recent violence in Mumbai and an impact of it led to violence in other parts of the country causing huge losses. *The Tribune* Editorial dated Oct. 24, 2008 has rightly exposed the Indian administration and observed: Marauding mobs manage to show such boorish behaviour because they know that the government does not have the courage to punish them for this kind of behaviour. They gain strength from the other side's weakness. If they know that they will have to pay for this crime, they would be better behaved. It is the government's responsibility to maintain law and order. In this connection, the ordinance that the Maharashtra government is bringing in is interesting. It makes it mandatory for perpetrators of violence to compensate for the loss of public property. It makes parties like the MNS accountable for damage to public property or face jail term. If implemented forcefully, it can drum some sense into the mobsters gone berserk.

Administration by itself may not be able to solve all the problems of natural and man-made disasters. Administration has to set example before the people with sincerity so that they become disciplined. R.P. Bhatia in his Article "Introspection For All" in *Hindustan Times,* (24th Oct., 2008) rightly observes, that as a man of 80, I have witnessed cycles of violence and civic madness. It grieves me, particularly in India, that we do not introspect enough, moderate our wants, behave fairly, share resources properly and do not cultivate our conscience. Whether we are believers, Agnostics or Atheists, we are all human and supposed to introspect. If we do so, the conscience inside will never allow us to harm others. He may be strong who conquers others, but he is truly mighty who conquers himself.

Notes and References

1. Nigro, E.A., "Public Administration: Readings and Documents", New York, Rinehart and Co. Inc., 1951.
2. White, L.D., Introduction to the Study of the Public Administration, Macmillan, 1955, p. 4.
3. *Ibid.*, p. 3

4. Whilson, Woodrow, 'The Study of Administration', *Political Science Quarterly*, 1941, pp. 481-566. Also in the *Political Science Quarterly*, Vol. 2, pp. 197-222, June 1887.
5. Pfiffner, Public Administration, The Ronald Press Company, N.Y., 1946, pp. 4-6.
6. *The Times of India*, 2.2.1993.

6

EARTHQUAKES AND TSUNAMIS

A. EARTHQUAKE

According to K.N. Khattri the outermost shell of the earth is fragmented into a mosaic of few large pieces called plates. These plates are able to move about relative to the interior of the earth as well as with respect to each other. As they move they jostle against each other and deform near their edge to Create Strains in the region. This strain ultimately results in the fracturing of rocks, creation of mountains and birth of earthquakes. Thus the morphology of the earthquakes is generally one of the narrow belts that circle the globe. Some of these traverse the continents in habited regions. In such regions, the mankind has been suffering the ravages of earthquakes from time to time.

Earthquakes, the very name of it, sends shock waves. Earthquakes cannot be predicted by any method available so far. On the one hand, we enjoy pleasures living on mother earth while on the other, we face its fury in the form of floods, fire, earthquakes, etc.

The earth experiences over a million earthquakes every year. Fortunately only a very small fraction of them, viz. a few dozen are strong enough to cause substantial damage and about a dozen of them are potent enough of inflicting heavy casualties and damage. Even so over the last four milliennia more than fifteen million people have lost their lives due to earthquakes. Thus they have come to be regarded as most dreaded phenomena by the humankind.

An Earthquake is a series of underground shock waves and movements on the earth's surface caused by natural processes writhing the earths crust.

Sanjay Narayan in his Editorial in *Business Today*, Feb. 21, 2001 says, that 'The cruelest truth about earthquakes is that while they last for mere seconds, the grim after-effects can go on for what can seem an eternity. Nearly two weeks after India's blackest Republic Day, when the Quake wrecked havoc in Gujarat in all of 45 seconds, business and Industry is still picking up the pieces in what is one of India's most Industrialized investment-friendly states. The true extent of the damage to business and industry in Gujarat will only unfold over the coming months, and the journey to rehabilitation will be a long and arduous one. But Gujarat is blessed with the indomitable spirit of entrepreneurship, something that its businessmen have amply demonstrated in India, as well as elsewhere in the world, notably in the US, it is this spirit that will undoubtedly help the state bounce back and claim its rightful place in the sun."

Earthquakes, the most feared of natural hazards as they occur without any recognizable warning, are unpredictable in space and time and inflict heavy losses in less than a minute duration.[1] A UNESCO study indicates that on an average 10,000 people die each year from earthquake and also result in losses amounting to billions of rupees.[2]

The power (energy) of an earthquake is reckoned in terms of its "Magnitude" which is measured on an open-ended Richter Scale from 1 to 8.9. But it is not a linear scale and not even a logarithmic scale. This will be clearly understood from the following Table 6.1 which gives the equivalence of earthquake magnitude (on Richter scale) and energy release by the explosion of a certain mass of TNT which is the well known measure of explosive power in any blast.

Earthquake classification on the basis of Richter Scale is as given in Table 6.1.

As per the vulnerability Atlas of India published by Building Materials and Technology Promotion Council,

TABLE 6.1

Earthquake Magnitude, Effects on Structures and Energy Released

[Based on the proposal by Richter, 1958 (2)]

Approximate Magnitude	*Effects of Shallow shocks in populated areas*	*Energy (ergs.) Year in the world*	*Number of Earthquakes per year*
8.0-	Damage nearly total	$10\text{-}24\text{-}10^{25}$	.1-0.2
7.4	Great Damage	10-23	4
7.0-7.3	Serious Damage-Rails Bent	$(2 \times 6) \times 10^{22}$	15
6.2-6.9	Considerable damage to buildings	$(0.1\text{-}1.4) \times 10^{22}$	100
5.6-6.1	Slight Damage to buildings	$(1.6\text{-}9) \times 10^{22}$	500
4.9-5.5	Felt by All	$(0.14\text{-}1.1) \times 10^{22}$	1,400
4.3-4.8	Felt by Many	$(0.18\text{-}1) \times 10^{19}$	4.800
3.5-4.2	Felt by some	$(0.11\text{-}1.2) \times 10^{18}$	30.000
2.0-3.4	Not felt but recorded	$(0.06\text{-}8) \times 10^{16}$	800,000

Source: GOI, Ministry of Home Affairs.

Ministry of Urban Development, GOI, New Delhi, 1997, the magnitude M of an earthquake is denoted by a number which is a measure of the energy released during the earthquake occurrence. It is now measured in different ways, the most commonly used is the Richter Scale according to which the magnitude of an earthquake is the logarithm to the base 10 of the maximum trace amplitude, expressed in microns, with which the standard short period torsion seismometer (with a period of 0.8 second, magnification of 2800 and damping nearly critical) would register the earthquake at an epicentral distance of 100 km. The scale being logarithmic, the energy of earthquake magnitude 'm+ l' is about 30 times the energy released in earthquake of magnitude 'm'. Magnitude scale is open ended, denoted numerically to one place of decimal (5.6, 8.3, etc.).

"The intensity of an earthquake at a place is a measure of the effects of the earthquake." A number of intensity scales have been in vogue in different times, namely, Rossi-Forel (RF), Modified Mercalli (MM), MSK 1964 and Japan Meteorological Agency (JMA) scales. All the scales are close-

Earthquakes

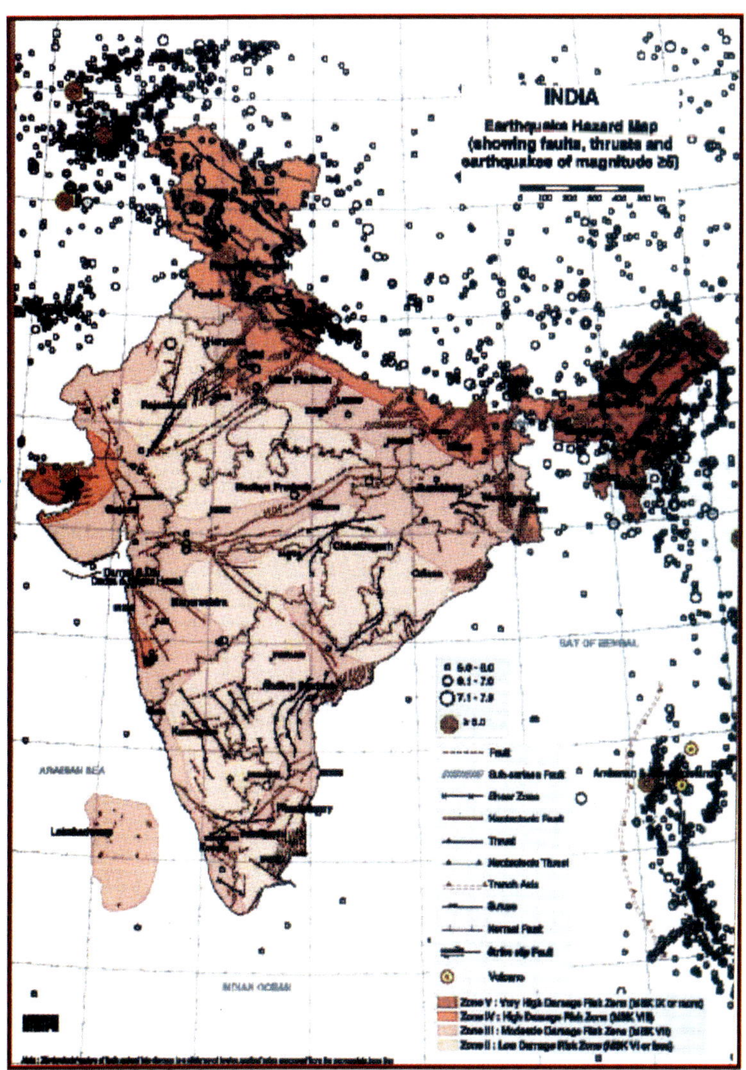

Source : Ministry of Urban Development, Nirman Bhawan, GOI, New Delhi.

ended stepped scales, RF having 10 points (I to X), MM and MSK with 12 points (I to XII) and JMA with 7 points (I to VII). Presently MSK 12 point scale is the most used, JMA being used in Japan. In historical earthquakes in India such as 1905 Kangra earthquake and 1934 Bihar-Nepal earthquake, RF intensity scale was used for drawing the isoseismal.

While for a given earthquake, the magnitude has one unique value and epicentral location, the intensity varies from the maximum in the epicentral area to smaller values at increasing distances from the epicentre. Isoseismal derived from the observed damages in an earthquake as per the intensity scale show the intensity distribution caused in the earthquake.

The relationship between the earthquake magnitude and the maximum intensity caused is not precise. Approximate relationship between them is shown in Table 6.2 below as a general guide.

Table 6.2

Approximate Relationships between M, MM Intensity and Felt Area

Earthquake magnitude richter, M	*Expected global annual number*	*Maximum expected intensity MM*	*Radius of felt area (km)*	*Felt area (km)²*
4.0-4.9	6,2000	IV-V	50	7,7000
5.0-5.9	800	VI-VII	110	38,000
6.0-6.9	120	VII-VIII	200	125,000
7.0-7.9	18	IX-X	400	500,000
8.0-8.7	1	XI-XII	800	2,000,000

Source: Earthquakes by Don de Nevi, Celestial Arts, Calif., May 1977, p. 102.

American geo-physicist James, N. Brunes visited India in March 1997. He made a clear-cut observation that there was a high probability of a great earthquake of magnitude 8.5 on the Richter Scale in the northern Indian subcontinent any time within the next 100 years. He warned planners, engineers and contractors involved in the building of dams and houses in areas above the Gangetic plains in the north. He predicted that damage expected after such great earthquakes would be much more devastating than in normal cases.[3]

Earthquakes, the very name of it, sends shock waves. Earthquakes cannot be predicted by any method available so far. On the one hand, we enjoy pleasures living on mother earth while on the other, we face its fury in the form of floods, fire, earthquakes, etc. Lyle Bavadam, in *Frontline*, Feb. 13-1, 2001, (p. 41) quoting Dr. P.P. Patel, Professor and Head of the Department of Geology at M.S. University, Baroda, feels that earthquakes send a forewarning. When Dr. P.P. Patel felt the tremors on the morning of January 26, his professional instincts told him that an earthquake with Bhuj, Bhavnagar or the Narmada Valley as the epicenter had occurred. An engineering, environmentalist and hydro-geologist, who has intimate knowledge of the Kutch region, Patel emphasized the fact that the earthquake could have been foreseen. "On December 27, there was an indication of heightened seismic activity. A minor earthquake measuring around 4 on the Richter scale occurred in Bhuj. It was ignored—it appeared as a small report in the Gujarati newspapers. Fearing renewed seismic activity, Patel organised a field workshop at the Bhuj Observatory in collaboration with the local administration and the Department of Science and Technology.

A. Earthquake Occurrences

India has large part of its land area liable to wide range of probable maximum seismic intensities where shallow earthquakes of magnitudes of 5.0 or more on Richter scale, have been known to occur in the historical past or recorded in the last about 100 years. IMD has prepared a catalogue of all such known earthquakes which is continually updated. The largest earthquake magnitude in India has been 8.7 which has its origin in the Shillong Plateau in 1897. This and the 1950 quake of M-8.6 in Sadiya region have been so intense that the rivers changed their courses, ground elevations got changed permanently and stones were thrown upward. A list of better known damaging earthquakes in India is given in Table 6.3

TABLE 6.3

List of Some Significant Earthquakes in India

Date	*Place*	*Toll*
1803	Garhwal	200 die
April, 4, 1905	Gangra valley (Himachal Pradesh) 8.0 magnitude	20,000 die
July 8, 1918	Assam, 7.6 magnitude	10,000 die
July 2, 1930	Dhubri (Assam) 7.1 magnitude	
January 15, 1934	Bihar and Indo-Nepal border, 8.3 magnitude	
June 26, 1941	Andaman Islands, 8.1 magnitude	532 die
Oct. 23, 1943	Assam 7.2. magnitude	
August 15, 1950	Assam, 8.5 magnitude	
July 21,1956	Anjar (Gujarat) 7.0 magnitude	
December 10, 1967	Koyna (Maharashtra) 6.5 magnitude	
January 19, 1975	Kinnaur (Himachal Pradesh) 6.2 magnitude	
August 21, 1988	Bihar and Indo-Negal border, 6.5 magnitude	1000 die
October 20, 1991	Uttar Kanshi (Uttar Pradesh) 6.6 magnitude	1500 die
September 30, 1993	Latur and Osmanabad (Maharashtra) 6.3 magnitude	7928 die
May 22, 1997	Jabalpur (M.P.) 6.0 magnitude	40 die
March 29, 1999	Chamboli (UP) 6.8 magnitude	150 die
Januray 20, 2001	Gujarat 6.9 magnitude	13811 die
Dec. 26, 2004	Tsunami A.P. and Tamil Nadu	136,132

Source: Compiled from Government documents.

Hazard Zones

As per the latest seismic zoning map of India the country is divided into five Seismic Zones. Zone V marked in red shows the area of Very High Risk Zone, Zone IV marked in orange shows the area of High Risk Zone. Zone III marked in yellow shows the region of Moderate Risk Zone and Zone II marked in blood shows the region of Low Risk Zone. Zone V is the most vulnerable to earthquakes, where historically some of the country's most powerful shock has occurred.

Geographically this zone includes the Andaman & Nicobar Islands, all of North-Eastern India, parts of north-western Bihar, eastern sections of Uttaranchal, the Kangra Valley in Himachal Pradesh, near the Srinagar area in Jammu & Kashmir and the Rann of Kutchh in Gujarat. Earthquakes with magnitudes in excess of 7.0 have occurred in these areas, and have had intensities higher than IX.

Much of India lies in Zone III, where a maximum intensity of VII can be expected. New Delhi lies in Zone IV whereas Mumbai and Chennai lie in Zone III. All states and UTs across the country have experienced earthquakes. (see map 6.1)

In recent times, the main city in Pakistan occupied Kashmir, Muzaffarabad was a scene of utter devastation after a magnitude of 7.6 earthquake struck on 8th October 2005, killing over 30,000 people across northern Pakistan.

Mega Cities and Danger of Earth Quakes

Mega cities are growing in India at a very fast rate without any regard to environment, feasibility and safety. A disaster in any mega city can create havoc in terms of loss in terms of human life, physical structures, money, material. It is high time to think of preparedness, prevention and mitigation efforts to protect our cities from the disasters that are likely to struck. We must follow the examples of Japan and California where disasters are frequent but without much damage. In the process of making cities disaster resilence, we have to put in proper place our urban local bodies who at the present times pass the building structures through corrupt practices. In addition, the personal engaged in urban local bodies are of inferior quality. Local bodies with the existing resources are finding it difficult to maintain basic services—potable drinking water and sewerage disposal. How can we expect from them to engage in activities for making cities free from disasters which require huge investments?

Asia has about half of all natural disasters, more than twice that of any other region in the world (Table 6.4).

Asia's high rates of urban and economic growth present policy-makers, planners, and investors with an opportunity to mitigate the potential impact of disasters. The number, size, and growth of Asia's cities indicate an increasing vulnerability to disasters. While the wealth created in urban centres could provide the means to address these potential risks through disaster mitigation strategies, little of this wealth is presently being diverted to the mitigation of disasters. Just as in many other parts of the developing

TABLE 6.4

Asia: The Most Disaster-Prone Region in the World

(Percentage)

	Number of Disasters	*Cyclones*	*Floods*	*Earth-quakes*	*Vol-canoes*	*Overall*
Asia	860	55	40	35	50	45
Pacific	123	15	—	—	10	6
Latin America	314	—	30	25	25	17
Caribbean	116	15	—	—	—	6
Africa	101	—	15	—	—	5
Europe	94	—	—	25	—	5
Near East	38	—	—	10	—	2
Rest of World	246	15	15	5	15	13
Disaster Worldwide	1890	770	675	375	70	100

Source: UNDP.

world, mitigation efforts that are underway are not of a sufficiently large scale to significantly reduce the growing vulnerability brought on by rapid growth.[4]

The Indian sub-continent is highly prone to natural disasters. Floods, droughts, cyclones and earthquakes are a recurrent phenomenon. As per the latest seismic zoning map brought out by the Bureau of Indian Standards (BIS), over 65% of the country is prone to earthquakes of intensity MSK VIII or more. Some of the most intense earthquakes of the world have occurred in India, but fortunately, none of these have occurred in any of the major cities. India has highly populous cities including the national capital of New Delhi, located in zones of high seismic risk. Typically, the majority of the constructions in these cities are not earthquake resistant. Thus any earthquake striking in one of these cities would turn into a major disaster.

It is most important in the medium and long-term to formulate strategies to reduce the vulnerability to and losses arising from a possible earthquake striking one of these cities. Six major earthquakes have struck different parts of India over a span of the last 15 years. The damages caused by these earthquakes reiterate the scale of vulnerability. However, if any of these earthquakes had struck populous urban centres, the damages in terms of human lives and property would have been colossal.

Frequent disasters lead to erosion of development gains and restricted options for the disaster victims. Physical safety—especially that of the vulnerable group—is routinely threatened by hazards. Disasters such as the Gujarat Earthquake have very clearly illustrated that we need mitigation, preparedness and response plans so that the threat to human life and property is minimized.

It is evident that the concept of disaster and environment management will dominate developmental programmes of the nations. The linkage between them is of significance because of their inter-dependence on each other. Urban population is more vulnerable to natural disasters on account of very high densities and locations of floods plains, coastal areas, seismic belts, etc. During the last century, the world has witnessed a considerable increase in losses due to natural disasters. Globally natural disasters account for 80% of all disaster affected people. Urbanisation is occurring at a very fast rate in areas where risks of natural disasters are greatest. 40 out of 50 fastest growing cities in the world are in earthquake zones. Another reason for larger risks in urban areas is due to destruction of eco-system. Due to high densities and lower availability of land, residents are forced to stay in high-rise buildings, which are highly vulnerable to deaths. People living in illegal squatter settlements in urban areas are also a reason of vulnerability.

It is estimated that in the next 40 years India will overtake China and become the most populous country of the world. New urban areas will have to be developed in adequate numbers to accommodate such a growth of urban population and to provide them basic civic amenities.

This growth threatens to make cities unsustainable because of the following:

1. The authorities have difficulty in providing basic services and as a result most of the population live in densely populated settlements;

2. Demand for land in cities has lead to use of unsuitable areas, which are prone to natural hazards;
3. Fast growing cities contain increasing number of poorly constructed buildings, which can lead to avoidable deaths. This fact is proved due to destruction by the earthquakes, which occurred in Latur, Uttar Kashi, Jabalpur, and Chamoli and cyclone in Andhra Pradesh and Orissa, Bhopal gas tragedy and Dabwali (Haryana) fire tragedy. It caused heavy losses not only to human lives but economic activities were also disrupted;
4. The concentration of hazardous materials and industrial complexes are increasing in urban areas, which put urban population at risks because in case of any natural hazard they will (cause secondary disasters such as fire, explosions, radiation, etc.); and
5. Urban development also increases the flood risk by disrupting natural drainage channels.

Capacity building for the technical/professionals persons is very important This should also include refresher courses. Communication channels and warnings are the most vital issues. Local authorities are required to establish the communication system for warning, evacuation and relief measures, etc. Local authorities are required to assist in management of post-disaster audits and can also reveal facts or weakness in present procedures. Last but not the least, resources including trained people should be organised and deployed where they will have the greatest effect. They should also prepare a list containing Do's and Don'ts for the information of general public. These lists should be displayed in all the local schools, offices, libraries, etc. They should also undertake mock exercises to make people aware of the steps to be taken in case of any such exigency. While the urban centers are contributing to the nation's economy they do not seem to have contributed towards creation of strong and efficient urban local bodies (ULBs) to derive them through. While the urban centers are growing, the ULBs have been degenerating.

The stakes are high given the enormous investment needs. Yet, regardless of the availability of financial resources, local government capacity to manage the delivery of services must be strengthened through improved planning and budgeting practices, and ability to draw on the private sector for service provision.

Increase in population of the cities is faster than their capacity to nurture them. This gap in demands of the urban growth and capacity of city systems to provide for them is increasing due to absence of or failure of policies to regulate the market mechanisms operating in the urban systems. Just like the economic sector, India thus needs reforms in urban management to solve the inefficiencies.

Among often forgotten, links between disaster and development are prevention and preparedness measures. Protective measures against the forces of nature is not self-evident. The question, therefore, arises as to how to protect people at large from disaster often at minimal additional costs. It can be done by way of management processes, training programmes, new building techniques, new understanding of how we interact with our environment.

The post-disaster activities are as follows:

1. Rescue;
2. Release
3. Repair;
4. Rehabilitation;
5. Reconstruction; and
6. Renewals

The immediate post-disaster activities can be formulated by giving assistance to the people, who have suffered a great loss by way of rescue, evacuation and provision of shelter; in shelters already built or by constructing temporary shelters if permanent are not available. It can also be (assistance) given by moving people to a safer place and by providing them basic amenities for example water, sanitation, food, health care, etc. and at the same time, protecting them from diseases and epidemics.

B. Earthquakes (Tsunami)

What is Tsunami?

Tsunamis are large waves that are generated when the sea floor is *deformed* by seismic activity, vertically displacing the overlying water in the ocean. Throughout recorded history, tsunamis have caused significant damage to coastal communities all over the world.

Tsunami is a series of large waves of extremely long wavelength and period usually generated by a violent, impulsive undersea disturbance or activity near the coast or in the ocean. When a sudden displacement of large volume of water occurs, or if the sea floor is suddenly raised or dropped by an earthquake, big tsunami waves can be formed by forces of gravity. The waves travel out of the area of origin and can be extremely dangerous and damaging when they reach the shore.

The word "tsunami" might have been only an Indian till December 26th, 2004, but today it is the most dreaded word for not only the victims of the killer wave but also everyone who cares about the misery of others.

It may have been a stranger for India but destructive tsunamis have occurred in all of the world's oceans and seas. In the last half of the 20th century, Pacific-wide, destructive tsunamis occurred in 1946, 1952, 1957, 1960, and 1964. Many more tsunamis occurred in inland seas around the periphery of the Pacific. These were extremely destructive locally and claimed thousands of lives. Such localized tsunamis occurred in 1975, 1983, 1985, 1992, 1993, 1995, 1998, 1999 and 2001. But none of them matched the fury of the 2004 killer.

The International Tsunami Information Centre, based in Honolulu, Hawai, has been educating the public about the threat from tsunami for the past many years.

By far, the most destructive tsunamis are generated from large, shallow earthquakes with an epicenter or fault line near or on the ocean floor. These usually occur in regions of the earth characterized by tectonic subduction along tectonic plate boundaries. The high seismicity of such regions is caused by the collision of tectonic plates. When these plates move, pat each other, they cause large earthquakes, which tilt, offset, or displace large areas of the ocean floor from a few kilometers to as much as a 1000-km or more. The sudden vertical displacements over such large areas, disturb the ocean's surface, displace water, and generate destructive tsunami waves. The waves can travel great distances from the source region, spreading destruction along their path.

It should be noted that not all earthquakes generate tsunamis. Usually, it takes an earthquake with a Richter magnitude exceeding 7.5 to produce a destructive tsunami.

Although relatively infrequent, violent volcanic eruptions represent also impulsive disturbances, which can displace a great volume of water and generate extremely destructive tsunami waves in the immediate source area. According to this mechanism, waves may be generated by the sudden displacement of water caused by a volcanic explosion, by a volcano's slope failure, or more likely by a phreatmagmatic explosion and collapse/engulfment of the volcanic magmatic chambers.

Less frequently, tsunami waves can be generated from displacements of water resulting from rock falls, icefalls and sudden submarine landslides or slumps. Such events may be caused impulsively from the instability and sudden failure of submarine slopes, which are sometimes triggered by the ground motions of a strong earthquake.

Major earthquakes are suspected to cause many under water landslides, which may contribute significantly to tsunami generation. In general, the energy of tsunami wave generated from landslides or rock falls is rapidly dissipated as they travel away from the source and across the ocean, or within an enclosed or semi-enclosed body of water such as a lake or a fort.

However, it should be noted, that the largest tsunami wave ever observed any where in the world was caused by a rockfall in Lituya Bay, Alaska on July 9, 1958. Triggered by an earthquake along the Fair-weather fault, an approximately 40 million cubic meter rock fall at the head of the bay generated a wave, which reached the incredible height of 520-meter wave (1,720 feet) on the opposite side of the inlet.

Tsunamis are disasters that can be generated in all of the world's oceans, inland seas, and in any large body of water. Each region of the world appears to have its own cycle of frequency and pattern in generating tsunamis that range in size from small to the large and highly destructive events. Most tsunamis occur in the Pacific Ocean and its marginal seas. The reason is that the Pacific covers more than one-third of the earth's surface and is surrounded by a series of mountain chains, deep-ocean trenches and/island arcs called the "ring of fire"—where most earthquakes occur (off the coasts of Kamchatka, Japan, the Kuril Islands, Alaska and South America). Many tsunamis have also been generated in the seas, which border the Pacific Ocean.

Once a tsunami has been generated, its energy is distributed throughout the water column, regardless of the ocean's depth. A tsunami is made up of a series of very long waves. The waves will travel outward on the surface of the ocean in all directions away from the source area, much like the ripples caused by throwing a rock into a pond.

The wavelength of the tsunami waves and their period will depend on the generating mechanism and the dimensions of the source event. If the tsunami is generated from a large earthquake over a large area, its initial wavelength and period will be greater.[5]

Tsunami more Powerful than Hiroshima Bomb

A leading Indian seismologist, Dr. J.G. Negi has calculated that the tsunami itself was 350 times more powerful than. the atomic bomb dropped on Hiroshima in 1945. He said that the energy released by the tsunami was to the tune of 5 mega-tone while the bomb that destroyed the Japanese City during World War II was of 15 kilo-tone only.

"What is more important," says Dr. Negi "is that the earthquake of Sumatra which caused the tsunami, itself had the power of 32,000 hydrogen bombs, considering that one hydrogen bomb has the power to release one mega-tonne energy. With the release of such huge amounts of energy, it is no wonder then that the tidal wave created the deadliest of all tsunamis ever. [6]

It resulted into more than one and a half lakh deaths, millions homeless and a great loss to property and danger of epidemics.

* Tsunamis are generated when the sea floor abruptly deforms and vertically displaces the water. When Tectonic earthquakes (earthquakes associated with the earth's crustal deformation) occur beneath the sea, the water above is displaced from its equilibrium position.
* Waves are formed as the displaced water mass, acting under the influence of gravity, attempts to regain its equilibrium. When large areas of the sea floor shifts, a tsunami can be created.
* As a tsunami leaves the deep water of the open ocean and travels into the shallower water near the coast, it transforms.
* The tsunami's speed diminishes as it travels into shallower water, its height grows. Because of this shoaling effect, a tsunami, imperceptible at sea, may grow to be several meters or more in height near the coast.
* When it finally reaches the coast, a tsunami may appear as a series of breaking waves.

Case Study: Tsunamis in Southern Asia—26th December, 2004.

The earthquake that shook Southern Asia on 26th December 2004 was one of the most powerful since the start of the 20th century, the US Geological Survey said. "We've just updated it to 8.9 magnitude. That makes it the fifth largest earthquake since 1990," said Julie Matinez, geophysicist from the US Geological Survey's (USGS) Earthquake Hazards Programme in Golden, Colorado. It was the largest quake in the world since 1964, she said. That year, a major earthquake hit Alaska's Prince William Sound.

It was a devastating earthquakes off the coast of Sumatra in the Indonesian artichpelago 81 Kms of Pulo Kunji, Great Nicobar, India and many countries of South Asia and East Africa—Indonesia, Sri Lanka, Thailand, Sonamia, Myanmar, Malivas, Malaysia, Tanzania, Bangladesh, Kenya, Seychells and including India where the Tsunami effected nearly 2200 Kilometers of the mainland coastlines, i.e. Tamil Nadu, Kerala, Andhra Pradesh and Pondicherry as well as Andaman and Nicobar Islands. This killer earthquake

(Tsunami) took a toll of over 2 lakh people, huge loss of property, injuries, loss of profession thus causing colossal social and economic miseries to coastal people, cutting a swathe of death and destruction across the coastal areas of a half dozens countries of the Indian Ocean, the titanic Tsunami rising from the fifth largest earthquake since the beginning of 20th Century—and the biggest in 40 years—has plunged the whole region in shock and grief on 26th December, 2004.

"These big earthquakes, when they occur in shallow water, . . . basically slash the ocean floor . . . and it's as if you're rocking water in the bathtub and that wave can travel basically throughout the ocean," USGS geophysicist Bruce Pressgrave said.

He said there had been no signs of the impending quake. "Unfortunately, we are not able to predict earthquakes at this time and one of the big reasons is typically these big earthquakes occur with no warning, no foreshock activity or anything like that", he added.

As the Earth moves and its plates hit each other, it breaks in one place and pressure builds up in a different area. When that pressure increases, another earthquake occurs. [7]

How it happened on 26th December, 2004

6.29 IST:

The India plate slips below the Burma plate and pressure builds up. Sudden movement of the plates causes earthquake with a magnitude of 9 on the Richter scale off the coast of Aceh province on the Indonesian island of Sumatra.

6.30 a.m.

Displacement of a part of the ocean floor forces the water upwards. A series of waves rushes outwards and races across the surface towards the shoreline. Quake of 6.1 mgnitudes felt in the Andaman at 8.30 a.m.

9. a.m.

As it nears the Chennai coast, the tsunami slows down but rises higher. It skims over the shallow water when it approaches the coast as it continues to gain height. The wall of water hits the shore with tremendous energy and leaves behind a trail of destruction. Once the tsunami hits land a part of its energy is defected back into the sea. This generates "edge waves" that travel back and forth.

TABLE 6.5

Human lives lost in the wake of Tsumani/Tide Wave in the Bay of Bengal—26th December 2004 (as on January 12, 2005)

Name of States/ U.T.	*Districts/ Islands*	*Population*	*Human lives lost*	*Total persons missing including fishermen*	*Persons moved to safer places*	*No. of Relief Camps/ Persons in the camps*
A & N	Bambooka	55	00	17	00	Evacuated
Islands	Car Nicobar	20292	466	491	7774	53/12984
	Chowara	1385	41	15	11	Evacuated
	Great Nicobar/ Campbell Bay	7566	102	16	1262	14/4328
	Kondul	150	38	—	200	Evacuated
	Kamorta	3412	48	390	312	4/1476
	Kathcal	5312	303	4354	269	3/3228
	Little Andaman	17528	50	15	4263	7/6569
	Little Nicobar	353	43	—	—	Evacuated
	Middle Andaman	54385	03	00	00	
	Nancowry	927	01	—	—	2/934
	Pilmillow	145	163	—	222	Evacuated
	Trinket	432	03	234	—	Evacuated
	Terassa	2026	50	9	—	9/3296
	South Andaman includes Port Blair	181949	05	—	3274	13/4330
	Strait Island	42	00	00	29	
	Total	295959	1316	5542	17616	105/37055
Andhra	Krishna	13061	27	—	—	—
Pradesh	Guntur	30700	12	—	—	—
	Nellore	16578	20			
	Parkasham	92547	35			
	West Godavari	2395	08			
	East Godavari	7836	03			
	Visakhapatnam	33203	00			
	Total	196320	105	11	34,264	People gone back. All 65 Relief Camps closed

Kerala	Kollam	600000	131			
	Allappuza	400000	35			
	Ernakulam	300000	5			
	Total	1300000	171	—	24978	29/24978
Tamil	Chennai	65322	206	—	30000	25/30000
Nadu	Cuddalore	99704	612	—	61054	38/24204
	Kancheepuram	100000	128	—	60000	/28792
	Kanyakumari	187650	824	—	46280	62/41250
	Nagapattinam	196184	6051	—	196184	96/91036
	Pudukotti	66350	15	—	4857	7/4857
	Ramanathapuram	6815	6		8350	6/8350
	Tirunelveli	27948	4	—	11170	20/11170
	Thoodhukudi	13072	3	—	13072	23/11625
	Thiruvallur	25600	29		15600	13/4700
	Thanjavur	24000	26		4600	13/4600
	Tiruvarur	NA	17		11295	21/11295
	Villupuram	78240	47		37500	14/37500
	Total	890885	7968		499962	412/309379
Pondi-	Karaikal	17432	484	66	15000	22/5200
cherry	Pondicherry	26000	107	9	55000	26/900
	Total	43432	591	75	70,000	48/6100
	Grand Total	2726596	10151	5628	646820	594/377512

Source: Ministry of Home Affairs, GOI, New Delhi.

CONCLUSION

Ajay Bagchi, in his article, "National Environment Policy", in *Pioneer*, Thursday, 30th December, 2004 observes:

"Hitherto ignored, ecology security is vital for our national security." However, the bottom line is the collective political and social will to safeguard our ecological security. We seem to ignore the truth that ecological security is as vital a component of our national security as the integrity of national frontiers. Even the most well crafted policy would not be of much help if the legal framework fails to take the prevailing social mores into account and the instruments of governance are not free to act according to law and are blunted by political interference. The crux of the problems relating to environmental damage in our country lies in unbridled greed and pervasive apathy of those who are in leadership positions in the country.

President APJ Abdul Kalam said that:

Beat nature's fury with humaneness.

I was born and lived in an island and I have witnessed

the islanders braving the fury of the sea during cyclones. This is the time, the one billion people must face the problem together as one nation and provide all support to all the needy states.[8]

Notes and References

1. R.K. Celly and T.N. Gupta, Dimensions of Natural Disaster Management in India, in *Shelter,* Dec. 13, 1999, p. 1
2. Ravi Shankar, Seismic Activity in India, *Shelter,* Dec. 13, 1999, p. 4.
3. Indian Science Congress Association, Presidential Address by Prof. Dlip Kumar Sinha, 1991, Indore, The Shaping of Indian Science, Indian Science Congress Association, Presidential Address, 2003, Vol. III, 1982-2003, p. 1729,.
4. David Hollister, Regional Development Dialogue, Vol. 15, No. 2, Autumn, 1994.
5. The Killer Called Tsunami, *The Tribune,* Chandigarh, Dec. 31, 2004.
6. Tsunami more powerful than Heroshima bomb, editorial in *The Times of India,* New Delhi, Friday, January 7th, 2005.
7. *The Tribune,* Chandigarh, Monday, Dec. 27th, 2004.
8. APJ Abdul Kalam, *The Pioneer,* Monday, 27th, Dec., 2004.

7

Cyclones

INTRODUCTION

'Cyclonic' Storms have been causing considerable damages to life and property in the coastal areas of India. They generally originate in the Bay of Bengal or the Arabian Sea during the pre-monsoon (April and May) and post-monsoon (October to December) seasons. However, the past data on occurrence of cyclones indicate that they are extremely rare in the winter months. The pre-monsoon and post-monsoon cyclones are, by and large of very great intensity, with inner cores of very strong wind velocity, reaching 100 kmph or even above. One of the severe cyclonic storms which struck West Bengal in October 1942 is said to be the most destructive with wind velocity which exceeded 150 kmph.[1]

The most destructive of weather systems, severe Tropical Cyclones (TC), brings worst disasters when it strikes coast in the preferred locations of the earth. Tropical cyclones are intense low-pressure areas with fierce winds blowing anti-clockwise manner in the Northern Hemishpere extending on an average 500 to 1000 km vertically. They are classified according to wind speed in their circulation. The associated winds often exceeding 200 kmps, rainfall exceeding 50 to 100 cm in 24 hours and worst of all, very high storm tide (storm surge combined with astronomical tide) often exceeding 5-6 meters brings disaster over the coastal areas in the wake of a cyclone. In extreme cases, with speed of 320 kmph gusting to 360 kmph, rainfall 120 cm in 24 hours and storm surge of 13-14 meters have been recorded in association with tropical cyclones. Out of these three destructive elements viz. strong winds, heavy rainfall and storm tide, the storm tide is responsible for 90 percent of the loss of life in the case of cyclone disasters. [2]

MEANING

Cyclone is a violent storm, often of vast extent, characterized by high winds rotating about a calm center of low atmospheric pressure. This center moves onwards, often with a velocity of 50 km an hour.

Cyclone is a relatively small and intense low latitude warm-core low pressure area having a wind circulation in clockwise direction in the Southern Hemisphere. The pre-requisites for the cyclones are:

1. Warm Ocean Temperature—above 27° celsius.
2. Absence of strong vertical wind shear.
3. Presence of Low pressure
4. Presence of Coricolis force.

A cyclone is a vast, violent whirl in the atmosphere which moves from the high seas towards the coastal area; its occurrence is confined to defined regions of the earth usually, in the tropical portion of the oceans. The havoc caused by cyclones is mostly due to strong winds, accompanied by torrential rains, tidal waves and the resultant inundation. The term cyclone is used to denote all tropical storms although they are known as Hurricane in the Atlantic and Eastern Pacific, Typhoon in Western Pacific, Willy-Willies in Australian sea, Baguis in the Philippines. In India, cyclones and tidal waves are common in eastern coast, on an average every year, one or two cyclonic storms lash the coastal districts. Cyclonic storms are sometimes accompanied by tidal waves with heights of five meters and sometimes hit 20 km. inland with wind speed of 150 kmph.[3]

Wind and Cyclones

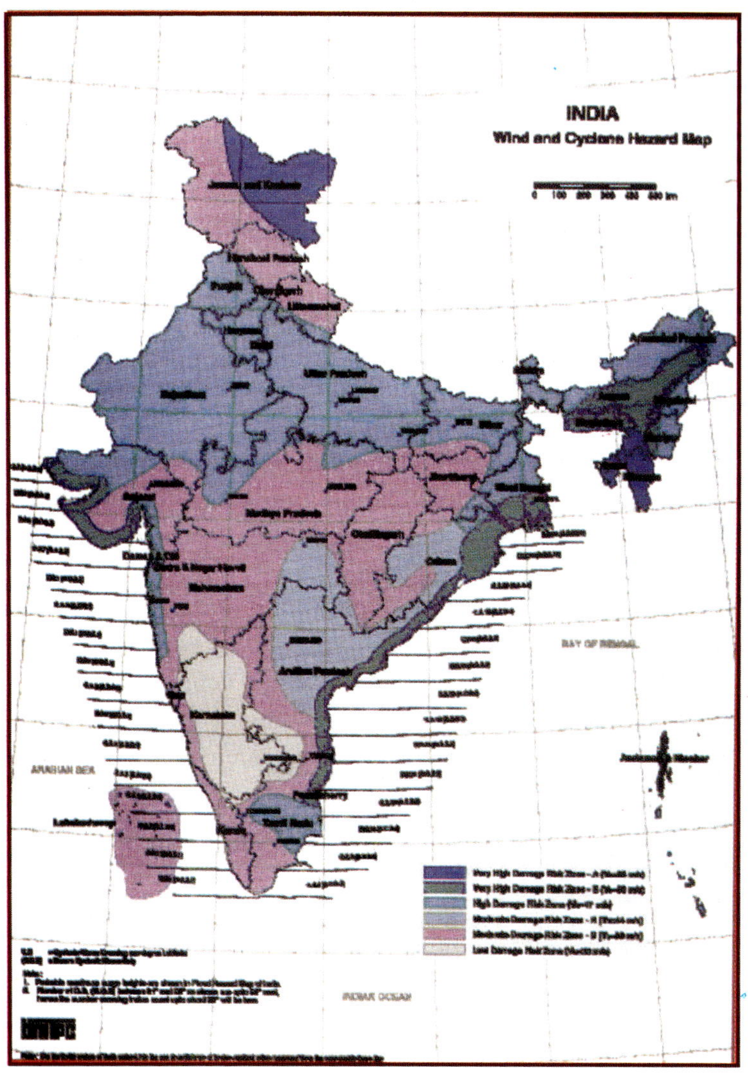

Source : Ministry of Urban Development, Nirman Bhawan, GOI, New Delhi.

ORIGIN OF CYCLONE

Cyclone originates in low pressure area when the sea surface temperature exceeds 27 degree centigrade. The heat makes the wind rise creating a vacuum in that place of the sea surface. To fill that vacuum, cool and heavy winds combined with rain move speedily to the sea surface. The coriolis force at the low latitude gives the cyclone its rotational or spinning motion. The "eye" of the cyclone is the center of the cyclone where the wind speed remains lowest. The radius of the "eye ball" ranges from 10 to 50 kms. The cyclone may approach at a speed of 350 kms. per hour and the rainfall exceeds 80 kms. in a few days. The cyclone surge may be at 8 meters at the coastal area and is called as the most severe cyclone. Cyclones mostly occur during the pre (April-June) and post (October-December) monsoon periods. Tropical cyclones at low latitudes accompanied by coastal strike coastal areas almost every year causing great havoc to/ the life and property.

TABLE 7.1

Types of Cyclone and Surface Winds

Sl. No.	*Type*	*Surface Winds*
1.	Depression	18 to 27 kts (6 to 54 kms per hour)
2.	Deep Depression	28 to 33 kts (56 to 66 kms per hour)
3.	Cyclonic Storm	34 to 47 kts (68 to 94 kms per hour)
4.	Severe Cyclonic Storm	48 to 63 kts. (96 to 117 kms per hour)
5.	Severe cyclonic storm with core of Hurricane winds	(>/117 kms per hour) (kms – Nautical Miles)

Source: Ministry of Home Affairs, Deptt. of Disaster Management.

CHART 7.1

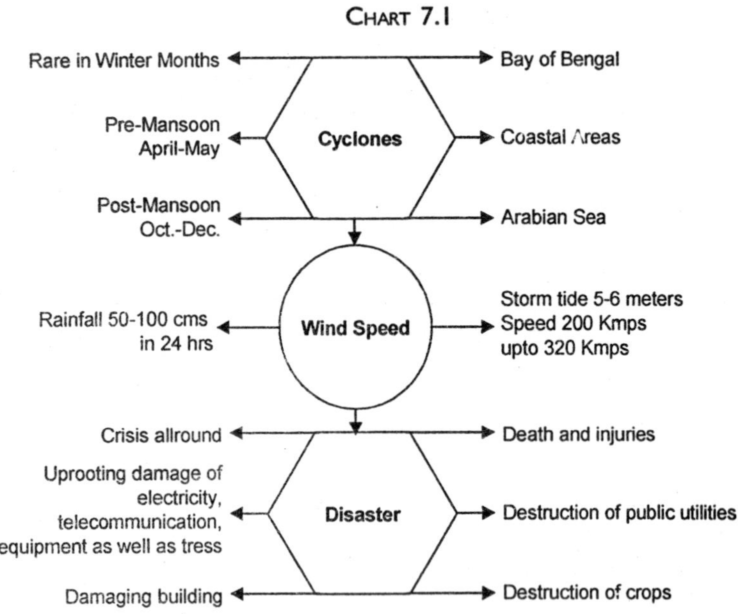

BASIC WIND SPEED ZONES

The macro-level wind speed zones of India have been formulated and published in 15:875 (Part 3), 1987 titled "Indian Standard Code of Practice for Design Loads (other than earthquakes) for Buildings and Structures, Part 3, Wind Loads". There are six basic wind speeds considered for zoning, namely 55, 50, 47, 44, 39 and 33 m/s. From wind damage view point, these could be described as follows:

55 m/s (198 km/h)	Very High Damage Risk Zone A
50 m/s (180 km/h)	Very High Damage Risk Zone B
47 m/s (169.2 km/h)	High Damage Risk Zone
44 m/s (158.4 km/h)	Moderate Damage Risk Zone A
39 m/s (140.4 km/h)	Moderate Damage Risk Zone B
33 m/s (118.8 km/h)	Low Damage Risk Zone

Infact, the cyclone affected coastal areas of the country are classified in 50 and 55 mls zones. The basic wind speeds are applicable to 10 m height above mean ground level in an open terrain.

The above basic maximum wind speeds in mls represent the peak gust velocity averaged over a short time interval of about 3 seconds duration. The wind speeds have been worked out for 50 years realm period with probability of excedence of 63%, based on the up-to-date wind data of 43 Dines Pressure Tube (DPT) anemograph stations and study of other related works available on the subject since 1964. The map and related recommendations have been provided in the Code with the active cooperation of Indian Meteorological Department (IMD).

In general, wind speed in the atmospheric boundary layer increases with height from zero at ground level to a maximum at a height called gradient height. The variation with height depends primarily on the terrain conditions. However, the wind speed at any height never remains constant and it has been found convenient to resolve its instantaneous magnitude into an average or mean value and a fluctuating component around this average value. The average value depends on the averaging time employed in analysing the ineterological data and this averaging time varies from a few seconds to several minutes. The magnitude of fluctuating component of the wind speed which is called gust, depends on the averaging time. In general, smaller the averaging interval, greater is the magnitude of the gust speed.

The basic wind-speed zones are plotted here in statewise maps which show the district boundaries as well as the district towns for their easy identification. Cyclones are classified according to wind speed.

The criteria followed by the Meteorological Department of India to classify the low pressure systems in the Bay of Bengal and in the Arabian Sea as adopted by the World Meteorological Organisations (WMO) are on next page.

COASTAL AREAS

As per the vulnerability Atlas of India published by Building Materials and Technology Promotion Council, Ministry of Urban Development, GOI, New Delhi, 1997, states that the coastal areas are subjected to severe wind storms and cyclonic storms. It is known that in certain events, the wind gusts could appreciably exceed the given basic wind speeds (by as much as 40 to 55%). But for design of structures and Probable Maximum wind speed in coastal districts is shown on the wind/cyclone hazard maps for East Coast. Similar data for West Coast needs to be computed, classification of vulnerability and risk to buildings, the above macro-level zoning is considered as sufficient.

The frequency of occurrence of cyclones on the different portions of the coast has been different. Even for the same design wind speed in some areas, the risk of damage per year will be higher in areas subjected to more frequent cyclones. Therefore, for the states having coastal areas, the number of cyclones having crossed the coastline from the year 1877 to 1990 has also been shown as cyclonic storm (C.S.) with wind speed between 34 and 47 knots and severe cyclonic storms (S.C.S.). Under the S.C.S. Category all cyclones with wind speeds greater than or equal to 48 knots have been included. It is to be noted that the cyclones crossing West Bengal coast shown on the map include those upto Longitude 90°E that is a part of Bangladesh coast.

CONCLUSION

Lessons may be taken after cyclone to avoid future cyclones or lessen their impact.

- Importance of Mangrove Plantation and its role in reducing the impact of cyclone.
- A need for dissemination of information upto the village level/vulnerable villages much ahead of time. (Alarming & warming system) Forcible eviction in advance.
- Need for a proper disaster-oriented insurance policy for all the vulnerable people and their assets in vulnerable areas.
- Incorporating rehearsal and demonstration classes to the community and particularly to the school children.
- Desalination of drinking water supply.

Types of Disturbances	*Associated wind speed in the circulation (1 knot = 1.85 km/hr)*
1. Low Pressure Areas	less than 17 knots (< 31 kmph)
2. Depression	17 to 27 knots (31 to 49 kmph)
3. Deep Depression	28 to 33 knots (50 to 61 kmph)
4. Cyclonic Storm	34 to 47 knots (62 to 88 kmph)
5. Severe Cyclonic Storm	48 to 63 knots (89 to 118 kmph)
6. Very severe cyclonic storm	64 to 119 knots (119 to 221 kmph)
7. Super Cyclonic Storm	120 knots and above (222 kmbh)

- A need for reaching safe drinking water during the flood and the cyclone period.
- A need for effective sanitation measures in villages.
- A massive awareness creation programme of Do's and Don'ts during cyclone/flood.
- Need for a better media management.
- Developing a people-oriented and need-oriented restoration of livelihood schemes.
- Need for community-based Disaster Management Programme. [4]

Crises are becoming a regular phenomenon at various levels. The leaders must learn to deal effectively with these crisis to keep the administration on an even keel. Crises are going to increase in future, as external and internal environments are under constant turbulence. There is a need to devise methods to deal with these crises in a planned and effective way. Crisis management system should be built in the administration of every organization.

Anurag Goel suggests that leaders must know methods to deal with a critical issue or situation which has become essential in the recent times. To quote him: The requisition of crisis management can be summed up as under:

TABLE 7.2

Brief History of Most intense Cyclones (in Particular from 1970-2001)

Date and Year	*Observed/ Estimated max. wind after landfall*	*Damage*
1	*2*	*3*
		OVER THE ARABIAN SEA
Oct. 19-24, 1975	180 kmph	85 people died in the districts of Junagadh, Jamnager and Rajkot of Gujarat state. This Cyclone caused considerable damage to property (estimated to be about Rs. 75 crores).
May 31-June 5, 1976	167 kmph	This cyclone caused damage to property which was estimated to be about Rs. 3 to 4 crores Burges each, Containing Rs. 5 lakh and 6 fishing boats were swept away. Mehsana, Bhavnagar, Kaira, Panchmahal, Rajkot and Broach districts of Gujarat State were most affected areas.
Nov. 12-13, 1977	167 kmph	Kerala and Laccadives were most affected areas due to this storm people killed, 72 houses damaged, 8400 and 620 fishing vessels damaged in Kerala coast. Total loss was estimated to be about Rs. 10 crores.
Nov. 5-13, 1978	278 kmph	Gujarat Cyclone Damage to property reported.
Oct. 28-Nov. 3, 1981	120 kmph	Junagadh, Rajkot and Jamnagar of Gujarat state were most affected areas. Total loss of damage to property was estimated to be about Rs. 52 crores.
Nov. 4-9, 1982	N/a	Saurastra coast of Gujarat about 45 km east of Veraval was affected very much by this storm, 507 people died and 1.5 lakh livestock perished.

1	*2*	*3*
Nov. 4-9, 1982	93 kmph	50 fishermen were reported missing in Gujarat Coast.
June 17-20, 1996	111 kmph	Severe Cyclone storm over the Arabian sea. As the system did not cross the coast. No significant damage was reported.
Oct. 23-28, 1996	111 kmph	Severe cyclonic storm over the Arabian Sea. As the system did not cross the coast. No significant damage was reported.
June 4-10, 1998	167 kmph	Gujarat and Rajasthan states were affected, Porbhander of Gujarat state was the most affected areas. Loss incurred due to storm was estimated to be about Rs. 1855.38 crores in Kandla.
May 16-22, 1999	195 kmph	This system caused severe damage in Kutch and Jamnagar district of Gujarat 453 people died. Loss of property estimated to about Rs. 80 crore. In Rajasthan one person died and 5104 cattle heads perished, 5133 houses were partially damaged.
		OVER THE BAY OF BENGAL
Oct. 1942	225 kmph	Over 10,000 people perished in the cyclone that hit Midnapore on October 15-14, 1942, during World War-II.
Nov. 8-13, 1970	224 kmph	Bangladesh Cyclone of which crossed Bangladesh coast in the night of 12th was one of the worst in recent times, with storm surges of 4-5 meters height at the time of high tides, and with 25 cm of rain in the areas the inundation took tool of about 2,00,000 people.
Oct. 26-31, 1971	185 kmph	Balasore (Orissa) 10,00 people died and 1 million people rendered homeless.
Nov. 14-20, 1977	259 kmph	Andhra Cyclones that crossed coast near Nizampatnam in the

1	2	3
		evening of 19th, took a toll of about 8,547 lives. The Ship Jagatswamini, which went right into the eye of the storm in the evening of 17th experienced maximum wind speed of 195 kmph. As the storm approached the coast, gale winds reached 200 kmph lashed Prakasam, Guntur, Krishna, East and West Godavari district, Storm surge of 5 meters high inundated Krishna estuary and the coasts south of Machilipatnam.
Nov. 9-14, 1984	213 kmph	Sri Harikota (A.P.) 604 people died.
Nov. 24-30, 1988	213 kmph	2000 people died, 6000 people missing in Bangaldesh.
Nov. 1-9, 1989	235 kmph	Kavali (A.) 69 people died.
May 4-9, 1990	235 kmph	Machalipatnam 967 people died.
April 25-30, 1991	235 kmph	Bangladesh 1,38,882 people died, 138,054 people injured.
April 24-May 2,1994	215 kmph	Bangladsh 184 people killed
May 15-19, 1997	230 kmph	Teknaf Bangladesh, 155 people died, 9663 people injured.
June 5-9, 1998	167 kmph	Kandla Cyclone, 1680 people died.
May 16-22, 1999	195 kmph	Arabian Sea, 454 people died and 5104 cattle heads perished in India.
Oct. 15-19, 1999	170 kmph	Gopalpur Cyclone—Orissa 198 people died, 402 persons injured.
Oct. 25-29, 1999	260 kmph	The Orissa Super Cyclone causec heavy destruction to coastal districts of Orissa, 9887 people died, 129.22 lakh people affected.
Nov. 26-30, 2000	189 kmph	Two states viz. Tamil Nadu and Pondicherry were mainly affected by this storm. The loss

(Contd.)

1	2	3
		is mainly due to crop damage. Uprooting of big trees and partial damages to more than one thousand kaccha house 30,000, Plantation trees and 50,000 plantain saplings got destroyed and 30,000 trees were uprooted in Tamil Nadu state. In Pondicherry two persons lost their lives damages to paddy crops plantation. Coconut plantation were the major loss in Pondicherry.
Dec. 23-28, 2000	167 kmph	Three districts of Tamil Nadu state were affected by this storm in the Ramnathapuram district. 350 houses were damaged in Thirunelveli. Houses damaged – 318. In Tutocoin houses damaged 318, Fishing boats lost 95, loss to crops 281 hectares paddy crops destroyed, plantain 650 hectares and betal 80 hectares.

Source: A Primer for Parliamentarians, Govt. of India, Ministry of Home Affairs, National Disaster Management Division.

(i) Identify the problems that could lead to a crisis and learn when and how to intervene most effectively.

(ii) Know how to carry out the difficult planning and coordination activities associated with preparing for, and managing, crisis.

(iii) Develop special negotiating and communication skills required to reduce conflict or ensure cooperation in a crisis situation.

(iv) Develop special knowledge and expertise in the field.

Crisis handling is both an art as well a science. It needs advance planning not to do it is to invite trouble and cannot be handled in a normal way. What is the result? Chaos and anarchy. We must not allow such a situation to occur.

Notes and References

1. Probable Maximum wind speed in coastal districts is shown on the wind/cyclone hazard maps for East Coast. Similar data for West Coast needs to be computed.
2. G.S. Mandal, Cyclones, The Problem Size, *Shelter, op. cit.*, p. 6.
3, Dr. Vijay Kumar, Cyclone Devastation: Its Implications, New Delhi, Serials Publications, 2005, pp. 1-2.
4. Source Book on District Disaster Management, Ministry of Home Affairs, GOI, LBSNAA, p. 229.

8

Flood Management

MEANING

In a document of the Ministry of Home Affairs, National Disaster Management Division entitled, "Hazards, Disasters and Your Community." Floods has been defined as: Floods is a temporary inundation of large regions as the result of an increase in reservoir, or of rivers flooding their banks because of heavy rains, high winds, cyclones, storm surge along coast, tsunami, melting snow or dam bursts.[1]

Even though the problem of floods has been receiving increasing attention and inspite of substantial investments in flood sector during the last few decades, it is observed that the flood damage in the country has continuously been showing a rising trend. It was in this context that the National Flood Commission was set-up in July 1976 by the Government of India to examine and advise on various aspects relating to floods. its report submitted in 1981, *inter-alia* laid great stress on proper floods plain management without diluting the importance of structural measures for specific situation. Subsequently, the specific problems of Ganga and Brahmaputra basins were also studied by high level committee of experts.[2] (See Table 8.1)

Rashtriya Barh Ayog (RBA) constituted by the Government of India in 1976 carried out an extensive analysis

CHART 8.1

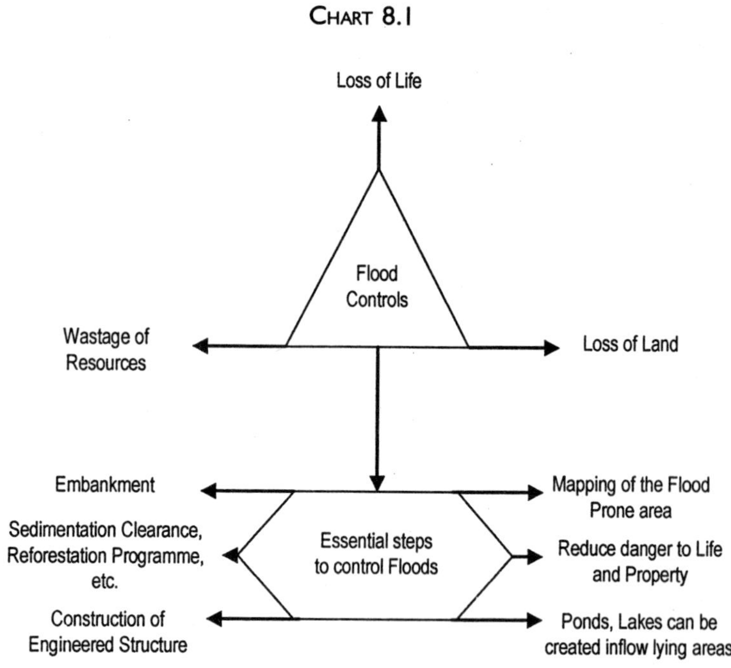

to estimate the flood-affected area in the country. RBA in its report (1980) has assessed the area liable to floods are 40 million hectares. It was determined by summing up the maximum area affected by floods in any one year in each state during the period from 1953 to 1978 for which data was analysed by the Ayog. This sum has been corrected for area that was provided with protection at that time and for the protected area that got affected due to failure of protection works during the period under analysis to arrive at the total area liable to floods in the country as per break-up given in Tables 8.2 and 8.3.

Flash Floods

Flash floods defined as floods which occurs within six hours of the beginning of heavy rainfall, and are usually associated with cloud bursts, storms and cyclones requiring rapid localized warnings and immediate response if damage is to be mitigated. Wireless network and telephone

TABLE 8.1

Area Liable to Floods in Different States

State	Area liable to Floods (million Ha.)
1. Andhra Pradesh	1.39
2. Assam	3.15
3. Bihar	4.26
4. Gujarat	1.39
5. Haryana	2.35
6. Himachal Pradesh	0.23
7. Jammu and Kashmir	0.08
8. Karnataka	0.02
9. Kerala	0.87
10. Madhya Pradesh	0.26
11. Maharashtra	0.23
12. Manipur	0.08
13. Meghalaya	0.02
14. Orissa	1.40
15. Punjab	3.70
16. Rajasthan	3.26
17. Tamil Nadu	0.45
18. Tripura	0.33
19. Uttar Pradesh	7.336
20. West Bengal	2.65
21. Delhi	0.05
22. Pondicherry	0.01
Total	33.516

Source: *Ibid*.

connections are used to monitor flood conditions. In case of flash floods, warning for timely evacuation may not always be possible. In a sudden development of severe heavy rain with heavy intensity in a limited place, torrential rain takes place causing sudden floods damaging human, plant and animal life. It causes land sliding and traffic obstructions.

MISUSE OF ALLOCATED FLOOD RESOURCES

Prof. Dilip Kumar Sinha in his Presidential to the Indian Science Congress at Indore in 1991, states that: Floods continue to be annual visitors in some parts of our country

TABLE 8.2

Area affected by Floods: Year-wise

Year	*Flood Affected Area (Million ha.)*	*Year*	*Flood Affected Area (Million ha.)*
1953	2.290	1954	7.490
1955	9.440	1956	9.240
1957	4.860	1958	6.260
1959	5.770	1960	7.530
1961	6.560	1962	6.120
1963	3.490	1964	4.900
1965	1.460	1966	4.740
1967	7.150	1969	4.740
1969	6.200	1970	8.460
1971	13.250	1972	4.100
1973	11.790	1974	6.700
1975	6.170	1976	11.910
1977	11.460	1978	17.500 (max)
1979	3.990	1980	11.460
1981	6.120	1982	8.870
1983	9.020	1984	10.710
1985	8.380	1986	8.810
1987	8.890	1988	16.290
1989	8.060	1990	9.303
1991	6.357	1992	2.645
1993	11.439	1994	4.805
1995	5.245	1996	8.049
1997	4.569	1998*	9.133
1999*	3.978	2000*	5.166
2001*	3.008	2002*	2.808

* Figures are tentative.
Source: Ministry of Home Affairs.

particularly in Andhra Pradesh, Bihar, Assam and West Bengal. There has not been a single year where a state exchequer in these states has not suffered a jolt for flood control. If someone goes through a newspaper report one is to find an interesting pattern of activities, etc. all of an *ad hoc* or piece-meal in nature initiated by Governments whatever be their complexion. Honestly speaking, these are least scientific. The doles might have benefited the affected community but

Floods

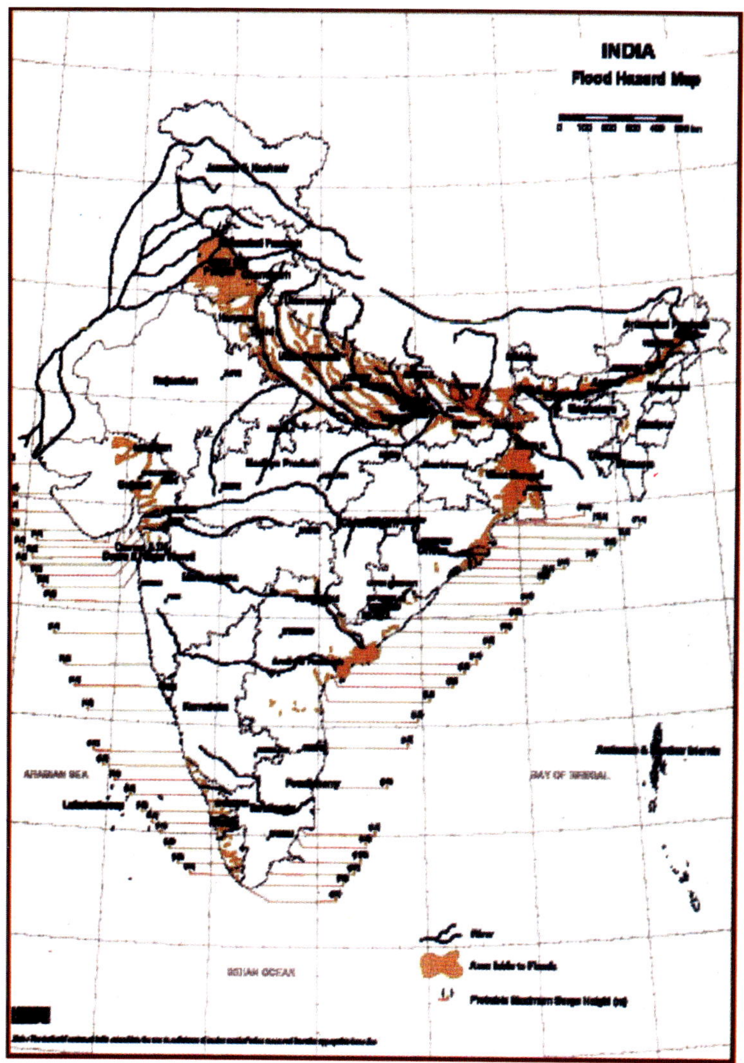

Source : Ministry of Urban Development, Nirman Bhawan, GOI, New Delhi.

TABLE 8.3

Maximum flood affected area from Data for the period 1953-78	34 million ha.
Add Area protected till then (1978)	10 million ha.
Deduct Area flooded due to failure of Protection works which might have been added in the reported flooded Area	4 million ha.
Total Flood Prone Area in the country	40 million ha.

Source: GOI: Ministry of Home Affairs, National Disaster Manufacture Division, p. 32.

one cannot say without any doubt that these have aided politicians to have a mileage and more so, when elections are in the offing. It would to be a travesty of truth if one sees nothing of a permanent nature either being done or having come into existence.[3]

Flash floods are characterized by very fast rise and recession of flow of small volume and high discharge which causes high damages because of suddenness. This occurs in hilly regions and sloping lands where heavy rainfall and thunder storm or cloud burst are common.

HYDRO METEOROLOGICAL CONDITIONS

Floods are recurrent phenomena in India from time immemorial. Almost every year some parts of the country or the other are affected by floods of varying magnitude. Different regions of the country have different climates and rainfall patterns and as such it is also experienced that while some parts are suffering under devastating floods, another part is suffering under drought. With the increase in population and developmental activity, there has been tendency to occupy the flood plains which has resulted in more serious nature of damage over the years. Because of the varying rainfall distribution, many a times, areas which are not traditionally prone to floods also experience severe inundation. Thus, flood is the single most frequent disaster faced by the country.

It has been estimated by the National Commission on Flood that the area prone to floods in the country was of the order of 40 million hectares, out of which 80%, i.e. 32 million hectares could be provided with reasonable degree of protection.

Floods are the most frequent natural calamity that India has to face almost every year in varying magnitudes in some or other parts of the country. The annual precipitation including snow-fall is estimated at 4000 Billion Cubic Metros (BCM). Out of this, the seasonal rainfall in monsoon is of the order of 3000 BCM. Rainfall in India is mainly dependent on the South-West and North-East monsoons, on cyclonic depressions and disturbances and on violent local storms. Most of the rainfall in India (80%) takes place under the influence of South-West monsoon between June to September (4 months). Remaining (20%) rainfall is received from North-East monsoon, cyclonic storm, local storms and cloud bursts. The rainfall in India shows great variations, unequal seasonal distribution, still more unequal geographical distribution and frequent departures from the normal. Normal annual rainfall varies from about 600 mm North-Western part to 2500 mm in North-Eastern part. It varies from 1200 mm in North (Bihar) to 2900 mm in the South (Kerala).

Table 8.1 depicts area liable to floods in different states. Table 8.2 explains the area affected by floods from 1953-2002.

CAUSES OF FLOODS

Flooding is caused by the inadequate capacity within the banks of the rivers to contain the high flows brought down from the upper catchments due to heavy rainfall. Flooding is accentuated by erosion and silting of the river beds resulting in reduction of carrying capacity of river channel, earthquakes and landslides leading to changes in river courses, obstructions to flow, synchronization of floods in the main and tributary rivers and retardation due to tidal effects. Some parts of the country mainly coastal areas of Andhra Pradesh, Assam, Orissa, Tamilnadu and West Bengal experience cyclones which often are accompanied by heavy rainfall leading to flooding.

Another cause for flooding has been the water logging in the irrigated area. This is due to excess irrigation water applied to command area and increase in ground water level due to seepage from canals and irrigated field. It has been assessed that an area of 2.46 m. is suffering from problem of water logging under irrigation commands in India.[4]

Flooding is mainly caused by:

(1) Inadequate capacity within the banks of the river to contain high flows,
(2) River bank erosion and silting of river beds,
(3) Land slides leading to obstruction of flow and change in the river course,
(4) Synchronization of floods in the main and tributary rivers,
(5) Retardation of flow due to tidal and backwater effects,
(6) Poor natural drainage,
(7) Cyclones and storm surge, and
(8) Cloud burst and flash floods.

REGIONS PRONE TO FLOOD IN THE COUNTRY

The rivers in India can be broadly divided into the following four regions for a study of flood problem:

(1) Brahmaputra Region;
(2) Ganga Region;
(3) North-West Region; and
(4) Central India and Deccan Region.

ORGANIZATIONS IN THE FIELD OF FLOOD MANAGEMENT

State Flood Control Departments

According to the policies evolved from time to time the primary responsibility for the management of floods rests with the respective State Governments. Schemes for flood management are investigated, planned and executed by the State Governments. According to the availability of funds and priority attached to each scheme, some States have departments of Irrigation and flood control, while in other States the Department of Irrigation is dealing with all activities related to management of floods in their respective areas.

Central Water Commission

In 1954, when for the first time the flood control programmer in the country attracted serious attention of the Government of India, a Central Flood Control Board was constituted. As per the decision of the Central Flood Control Board in 1954, a Flood Wing was added to the then Central Water and Power Commission; the Flood Wing served as the Secrètariat of the Central Flood Control Board.

The River Management Wing (RM) of the Central Water Commission is now headed by a member. This organization functions as an apex body on flood management in the country. Some of the major functions of the RM Wing of Central Water Commission are:

(i) To provide guidance in the preparation and scrutiny of flood control schemes, draft master plans and flood/drainage/anti-water-logging aspects of multipurpose projects.
(ii) Planning and operation of hydrometric and flood forecasting systems.
(iii) To coordinate and act in liaison with various authorities in processing and execution of flood control, irrigation, drainage and hydro-electric schemes in the Union Territories and States.
(iv) Guiding the Damodar Valley Corporation for reservoir management.

The organization has served as an expert technical body to render consultancy and assistance to States in flood management. A number of inter-state Committees, e.g. the Lamina Committee, etc. have been functioning under its active guidance. It is also providing flood forecasting and warning service for 171 stations in all major inter-state river systems spread over 62 sub-basins.

APPROACHES, POLICIES AND MEASURES

Approaches

The approaches to deal with floods may be anyone or more combination of the following available options:

(i) Attempts to modify the flood.
(ii) Attempts to modify the susceptibility to flood damage.
(iii) Attempts to modify the loss burden.
(iv) Bearing the loss.

EVOLUTION OF POLICIES ON FLOOD MANAGEMENT IN INDIA

After the unprecedented floods of 1954, the Government of India took several initiatives and constituted a number of Committees to study the problem of floods in the country. The important steps are:

- Policy Statement, 1954.
- High Level Committee on Floods, 1957.
- Policy Statement of 1958.
- Ministerial Committee on Flood Control, 1964.
- Minister's Committee on Floods and Flood Relief, 1972. Working-Groups on Flood Control for Five Year Plans.
- Flood Management: Case Studies
- Rashtriya Barh Ayog (RBA), 1980.
- National Water Policy (1987).
- National Commission for Integrated Development Plan, 1996.
- Regional Task Forces, 1996.
- National Water Policy (2002).

There are certain measures which can be taken for mitigating the damage caused by floods. Structural measures. Inspite of increased outlay for flood management sector, the state governments are reporting increased: (a) area of inundation; (b) affected population, (c) damage to crops, (d) damage to houses; and (e) damage to public utilities with increasing population pressure, it is but natural to expect further encroachment and consequent development of flood plains. While encroaching and utilizing the flood plains, the right way of the river on its plains for passage of floods many have to be accepted and the extent of utilization would have to be in keeping with our capability to pay the natural tax.

Unstructured Approach

During the earlier period there has been much dependence on structural measures under the approach of modifying the floods. As structural measures alone have not given desired results and flood damages continue to show increasing trend, non-structural measures such as flood forecasting, flood plain zoning, flood proofing of civil amenities of the affected villages, changing the cropping pattern and public participation in flood management works should be given fair trial as suggested under the other two approaches. These measures are more cost and time effective and they would go a long way in tackling the problem of floods more effectively.[5]

P.17, Second Administrative Reforms Commission, GOI, in its Third Report, "Crisis Management From Despair to Hope", Sept. 2006 mentions the following (based on National Water Policy):

- There should be a master plan for flood control and management for each flood prone basin.
- Adequate flood-cushion should be provided in water storage projects, wherever feasible, to facilitate better flood managements. In highly flood prone areas, flood control should be given overriding consideration in reservoir regulation policy even at the cost of sacrificing some irrigation or power benefits.
- While physical flood protection works like embankments and dykes will continue to be necessary, increased emphasis should be laid on

non-structural measures such as flood forecasting and warning, flood plain zoning and flood proofing for the minimization of losses and to reduce the recurring expenditure on flood relief.

- There should be strict regulation of settlements and economic activity in the flood plain zones along with flood proofing, to minimize the loss of life and property on account of floods.
- The flood forecasting activities should be modernized, value added and extended to other uncovered areas. Inflow forecasting to reservoirs should be instituted for their effective regulation.

CONCLUSION

Following steps can improve flood control:

- Mapping of the flood prone areas is a primary step involved in reducing the risk of the region.
- Land-use control will reduce danger of life and property when waters inundate the floodplains and the coastal areas.
- In Urban areas, water holding areas can be created in ponds, lakes or low-lying areas.
- Construction of engineered structures in the flood plains and strengthening of structures to withstand flood forces and seepage.
- Sedimentation clearance, reforestation programme, dike and flood wall construction can be taken as part of the community-based mitigation programme.

Notes and References

1. Presidential Addresses to the Indian Science Congress, 1991, Indore, published on the Shaping of Indian Science, Indian Science Congress, Association Presidential Addresses, Vol. III: 1982-2003, Universities Press, pp. 1736-37.
2. B.S. Ahuja, Dimensions of the Problem-Floods in *Shelter, op. cit.*, p. 5.

3. Presidential Addresses to the Indian Science Congress, 1991, Indore, published on the Shaping of Indian Science, Indian Science Congress, Association Presidential Addresses, Vol. III: 1982-2003, Universities Press, pp. 1736-37.
4. See foot note of Vol. 2.
5. P.C. Jain, "Flood Mitigation Practices in India", Disaster Management, National Centre for Disaster Management, 1999, pp. 45-46.

9

DROUGHT

INTRODUCTION

Drought is slow onset natural hazard and it offers time and opportunity to mitigate its impact. The droughts can be grouped on the basis of physical characteristics and their impact on socio-economic system both in time and space:

Meaning

Definitions of Drought thus vary widely with the area of interest. Many definitions are available of drought as given below:

- Palmer (USA) defines drought as an interval of time, generally of the order of months or years in duration, during which the actual moisture supply at a given place consistently falls short of the climatically expected moisture supply.
- The US Weather Bureau defines drought as a period of dry weather of sufficient length and severity to cause at least partial crop failure.
- National Oceanic and Atmospheric Administration defines agricultural drought as a combination of temperature and precipitation over a period of several months leading to a substantial reduction in yield (bushels per acre) of one or more of the

CHART 9.1

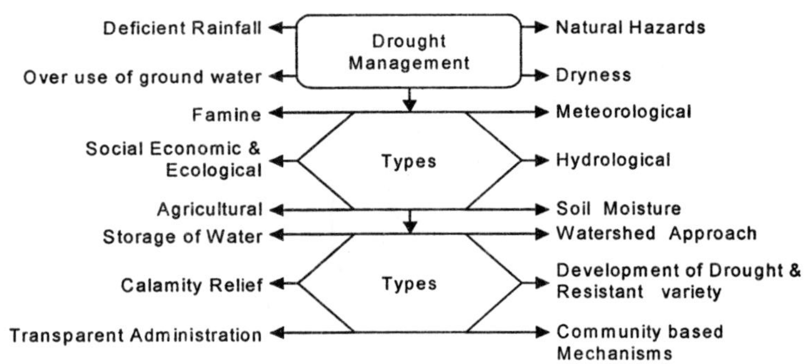

major food grains (wheat, soyabean, corn). A "Substantial reduction" is defined as a yield (bushels per acre) less than 90% of the yield expected with temperature/precipitation equal to long-term average values.

- Thornthwaite defines drought as a condition in which the amount of water needed for transpiration and direct evaporation exceeds the amount available in the soil.
- According to the British Rainfall Organization a partial drought is a period of more than 28 days with a very small rainfall per day and absolute drought is a period of at least 15 consecutive days during which the rain does not exceed 0.25 mm.
- The objective method for specifying drought suggested by the Australian Bureau of meteorology is to specify the minimum water need for a particular purpose. Drought occurs when rainfall during an interval is less than the minimum water need.
- In USSR drought is defined as a period of ten days with a total rainfall not exceeding 5 mm.

A generally accepted definition of drought is a temporary reduction in water or moisture availability significantly below the normal or expected amount for a specified period. The key assumptions of such a definition are:

(i) The reduction is temporary (if the reduction were permanent then terms such as "dry" and" arid" would be more appropriate),
(ii) The reduction is significant.
(iii) The reduction is defined in relation to a "norm", i.e. normal expectation, and the period taken as the basis for the norm is specified.

Jatinder Kumar Sinha defines drought as: Drought is a natural hazard generally caused by deficient rainfall and overuse of ground water. To mitigate its effects a suitable mix of policy reforms, Institutional changes and technology options is needed. Storage of water, rainwater harvesting, watershed approach to rain fed farming and development of drought resistant crop varieties are some steps to effectively check the impact of drought.

Drought indicates dryness or want of rainfall or water. As the total rainfall decreases, the tendency to both spatial and temporal variation in rainfall increases. In fact, if the rainfall tends to decrease by more than 30% over the mean, those areas are classified as drought-prone. The World Bank reported 60 million hectares (mha) in about 72 districts as drought-prone in India. In any case, drought effect could be up to 50% crop loss.

K.S. Narayana and Delina, in their article, "Natural Disasters and Voluntary Action", in *Moving Technology*, June 1992, observe that drought is the result of insufficient and untimely rainfall because of the soil erosion. Rainwater runs off quickly instead of getting absorbed in the ground, thereby reducing the moisture content. Our neglect of environment is having disastrous consequences and the damages are largely irreversible. The root of the problem of the drought is the ecological destruction. Deforestation speeds up the process of desertification.

Impact: Drought as one of the major natural calamities has posed big threat to the food security and elimination of poverty and hunger all around the world, especially within our own country. Management of drought is, therefore, a major concern in the domain of our Disaster Administration. Coping with this natural malady requires extensive planning, presentation and management entailing willing and active participation of role players from diverse segment within the Government and outside.

Drought though less spectacular in its fury is a lingering disaster which ravages some part of the country or the other, following local deficiencies in rainfall. There have been occasion when the impact of drought has been so wide-spread as to make it a mater of national concern. This happened in 1987-88, 1990-91 and more recently in 2000-2001.

Drought impacts mostly rainfed crops to start with and subsequently the irrigated crops. Areas with minimum of alternative water sources to rainfall (ground and canal water supplies), areas subjected to drastic environmental degradation such as denuded forest lands and altered ecosystems, and areas where livelihoods alternative to agriculture are least developed are most vulnerable to drought. The herdsman, landless, laborers, subsistence farmers, the women, children, and farm animals are the most vulnerable groups affected by the drought conditions.

DRAUGHT CONDITIONS

- Deficiency in rainfall of 25% and above where the annual normal rainfall is more than 1000 mm, 20% and above where the annual normal rainfall is above 750 mm to 999.9 mm and 15% and above where the annual normal rainfall is less than 750 mm.
- Crop loss of 50% and more as per eye estimation survey for normal crops. In case of high input oriented crops like groundnut, bengal gram, hybrid sunflower, etc. reduction in the yield of 40% and above.
- Compression/reduction in the cropped areas of 50% and above under all principal crops.
- Dry spells and its impact on crop damage.
- The estimated anna valuation of crops in the area

with actual anna valuation during the two preceding years.

- Sudden rise in prices of food grains and fodder.
- Failure of crops and fodder and the extent thereof.
- Shrinkage of water level in wells and tanks.
- Sudden fall in rates of wages of labour.
- Sudden unusual movement of labour in search of employment.
- Sudden migration of cattle.
- Malnutrition among children and other vulnerable section of the society.[1]

Classification

* *Meteorological drought*: A situation arising from inadequate and mal-distribution of rainfall;
* *Hydrological drought*: Conditions denote reduced stream flow and inadequate filling of reservoirs, tanks or drying up of water in the surface water storage structures;
* *Soil moisture drought*: Inadequate soil moisture particularly in rainfed areas which may not support crop growth;
* *Agricultural drought:* Characterised by low soil moisture levels and shortage of water resulting in crop failures;
* *Socio-economic drought:* The reduction of availability of food and income loss on account of crop failures endangering food and social security of the people in the affected areas;
* *Famine:* When large scale collapse of access to food occurs which without intervention, can lead to mass starvation; and
* *Ecological drought*: When the productivity of a natural eco-system fails significantly as a consequence of distress induced environmental damage.[2]

The transition from meteorological drought to hydrological drought and then on to agricultural drought may be termed as early drought onset phase. This phase is characterized by low water storage in reservoirs, poor recharge of ground water aquifers, mostly in irrigated areas and inadequate soil moisture primarily in rainfed areas, to support crop growth, constitute the basic consequences of drought. The progression from agricultural drought to socio-economic drought causes famine situation constituting ultimate consequence of drought when community progressively loses its exchange entitlements to food and productive assets. At this late stage, distress induced environmental degradation forces affected communities to take recourse to cutting down vegetative cover to cope with acute food shortages. The situation also results in land degradation and sharp fall in livestock population upsetting the energy cycle of eco-system.

THE DROUGHT PROFILE

India, due to its geographical location and climatic conditions which vary widely across the country, is susceptible to various natural disasters including Drought in spite of having a normal monsoon for the last 13 years, one or another part of the country has experienced drought or drought-like situations. There are some parts which are perennially prone to drought due to the climatic conditions associated with very low rainfall and consequential chronic moisture distress. While other parts experience drought conditions on account of untimely, erratic or less than normal rainfall during the Monsoon period (1st June to 30th September in case of South West Monsoons and December and January in case of North-South Monsoons).

Our country has a geographical area of 328.7 million hectares. Out of this, the net area sown is 142.2 million hectares as per the latest available statistics. The net irrigated area is approximately 55.1 million hectares which means that in approximately 87.7 million hectares or 61.67 percent of the cropped area, farming is entirely dependent on rainfall barring some supplementary irrigation which may be available from local sources. The distribution of the sown area under various ranges of rainfall is as under:

(a) 33 per cent	Low rainfall region—750 mm or less
(b) 35 per cent	Medium rainfall region—750-1,125 mm,
(c) 24 per cent	High rainfall region—1,125-2000 mm,
(d) 8 per cent	Very high rainfall region—2000 mm or above.

Due to erratic behaviour of the Monsoon, even the medium rainfall region is vulnerable to drought conditions. As such, about 68 per cent of the sown area is prone to drought of varying degrees at one time or the other.

As per a study carried out by Central Water Commission (CWC), 99 Districts were identified as prone to drought conditions. CWC adopted a smaller Unit viz. Talukas for drought identification studies instead of Districts and 315 Talukas out of a total of 725 Talukas in these 99 districts were thus identified. Through this more focused exercise, it is possible to demonstrate that 51.12 Million Hectare out of 108 Million Hectare being the area of these Districts is actually drought prone.

It may, however, be clarified that generally the trend is to shift to Talukas or Tehsils rather than District as the geographical unit for declaration of drought. Vulnerability of districts in the country to drought has also been worked out through different instrumentalities e.g., India Meteorological Department, the erstwhile Irrigation Department (now the Ministry of Water Resources), Planning Commission and the Bagchi Committee, etc. In all, 246 districts have thus been identified by one or the another Department/Committee, using different criteria for different purposes.

Statistically in the recent past around 15.55% area of the country can be said to be perennially drought prone. The magnitude of some of the recent widespread droughts can be had from the following:

As occurrence of drought is the product of inter-play between Meteorological, Agricultural and Hydro-geological factors, the responsibility of determining whether a particular area is affected by drought rests with the State Governments.[3]

TABLE 9.1

Year	No. of States	No. of Districts	No. of Villages	Cropped area (in lakh ha.)	Human Population (in lakhs)	Animal Population (in lakhs)
1987-88	21	263	2.55,837	586.00	2854.19	1681.11
1999-00	11	125	N.A.	134.22	369.88	345.60
2000-01	9	170	11 0982	210.73	1674.35	692.99
2001-02	5	103	22,255	67.44	88.19	34.28

Source: Ministry of Agriculture, GOI, New Delhi.

Impact

Drought, different from other natural disasters, do not cause any structural damages. The typical effects include loss of crop, dairy, timber (forest fires), and fishery production; increase in energy demand for pumping water, reduced energy production; increased unemployment, loss of biodiversity, reduced water, air, and landscape quality; groundwater, depletion, food shortage, health reduction and loss of life, increased poverty, reduced quality of life, and social unrest leading to migration.

Drought impacts mostly rainfed crops to start with and subsequently the irrigated crops. Areas with minimum of alternative water sources to rainfall (ground and canal water supplies) areas subjected to drastic environmental degradation such as denuded forest lands and altered ecosystems, and areas where livelihoods alternatives to agriculture are least developed are most vulnerable to drought. The herdsman, landless labourers, subsistence farmers, the women, children, and farm animals are the most vulnerable groups affected by the drought conditions.[4]

Remedies

Jitendra Kumar Sinha, in his article, "Causes of Drought and Remedies", in *Kurukshetra,* September 2000, observes that a holistic approach encompassing a suitable mix of policy reform, institutional changes and technology options is needed to achieve longer term immunity which may comprise of the following:

1. Storage of water.
2. Utilization of surplus water in the water deficit areas.
3. Watershed approach to rainfed farming.
4. Water pricing reflecting opportunity costs.
5. Community-based mechanisms to regulate ground water.
6. Development of drought resistant varieties.

Every drought teaches some lessons and they remain invariably the same. Then also, same mistakes are repeated. Follies of the past are forgotten very quickly. It is true that the country is ultimately able to tide over any crisis. This is the inner strength of the Indian democracy. M Prof. Amartya Sen said, only democracies had the in-built protective systems that prevent famines. That is why even in our greatest crises, we have had no famines since independence, but China has suffered acutely. But, there should be no scope of complacency.[5]

Main mitigation Strategies

1. Drought Monitoring,
2. Water supply augmentation and conservation—Watersheds,
3. Land use,
4. Livelihood Planning,
5. Drought Planning, and
6. Public awareness and Participation.

CONCLUSION

Presently, there is a fine institutional mechanism, connecting central and state governments all the way to the district level on the delivery of drought relief services. This system has been instrumental in preventing famines, in safeguarding livelihood systems, and in ensuring their recovery. The effective and efficient utilization of climate information products and institutionalizing decentralized climate variability risk management approaches require institutional arrangements that connect the climate information providers and intermediary resource and policy institutions with community-based institutions including end users such as farmers. End to end climate application systems for climate variability management does not currently exist in India.

Currently, the generated climate information products only cater to broad policy-making at the macro-level on the one hand, or are at the fine scale of the weather. As a result, the intermediary scaled climate events, ranging from several weeks to seasonal and inter-annual, important to a variety of climate-sensitive decisions and policies, are not being put to use for resource management at the community, local and state levels. This gap needs to be addressed setting up a coordinated institutional system that connects the demands and applications of climate information products at various levels including local community, district, state and national levels. The generation of timely climate information products that are demand driven, being particular to the needs of decision-makers at various levels and being contextually specific to the needs of the ecological and socio-economic systems.

There needs to be an institutional arrangement with a comprehensive climate variability management and dynamic responsive planning. At the national level institutional mechanisms over the decades have evolved into a good integrated system to monitor the development of the monsoon and to observe and report on the macro-impacts of the unfolding monsoon primarily on agriculture production. In Karnataka, an important addition is being made to integrate critical climatic indicators with agricultural and water resource management by the Drought Management Cell. The mechanism in Karnataka facilitates in reporting observed climatic phenomena at sub-state levels and on the unfolding impacts. This helps in undertaking quick response interventions. The mechanism in Karnataka is able to assess drought impacts at sub-state levels and provide policy-makers with much needed data to help facilitate response to differential impacts at finer scales. However, the institutional infrastructure is not utilizing climate information(s) in the range of weeks to seasonal scale as well as draw climate variability patterns from the past climate data for guiding development and mitigation planning. The system is yet to incorporate livelihood system, vulnerability dynamic parameters to climate risks and rely mainly on bio-physical parameters. As a result of this critical gap, anticipatory (risk) management is not being practice even in Karnataka.

In consonance with adoption of climate variability management approach, there is a need to redesign institutional arrangements at the Local/District/State/National levels with a capacity to track parameters relating to climate and the societal systems on a continuous basis regardless of occurrence of drought to guide policy-making and programme implementation to anticipate and manage climate risks instead of responding to crisis situations, the study of history of Indian drought management reveals that India had always capitalized on the lessons from drought management in the past to refine and manage subsequent droughts effectively. It is hoped that the 2002 drought management lessons also could be synthesized and assimilated into the system to refine management practices, while 1965-66 drought management experiences eliminated the word "famine", 1972-73 drought management experiences made the word "scarcity" redundant, the 1979-80 and 1987-88 drought management practices incorporated the word "Drought Management" and the 2002 drought is likely to set in motion "Climate Variability Management." By incorporating "Climate Variability Management", it is hoped that the fundamental change would usher a new paradigm from 'in-situ' drought management to 'in-situ' resource management, replacing resource transfer from distant places with resource generation and conservation measure within the affected zones.[6]

Notes and References

1. S.K. Swami (ed.), Drought Management in India, Ministry of Home Affairs, GOI, New Delhi, 2002, p. 32.
2. A.R. Subbiah, Drought Management Through Anticipatory Multi-dimensional Approaches: A Case Study, in Vinod Sharma, *op. cit.*, p. 92.

3. S.K. Swami, *op. cit.*, pp. 1-3.
4. GOI, Ministry of Home Affairs, National Disaster Management Division, Hazards, Disasters Your Community, New Delhi.
5. *Ibid.*, pp. 91-100.
6. A Report, Department of Agriculture & Cooperation, Ministry of Agriculture, GOI, Drought 2002, pp. 186-87.

10

Accidents—Roads, Railways, Air, Building Collapse

INTRODUCTION

India has a vast road network of 3.32 million km. of which the National Highways and the State Highways together account for 1,95,000 km. Though the 58,112 km. National Highway network, which is the responsibility of this Ministry, comprises only 1.75 per cent of the total length of roads, it has to carryover 40 percent of the total traffic across the length and breadth of the country. The strain on the network is increasing everyday. The number of vehicles has been growing at a rapid pace of 12 per cent per annum over the last few years and, consequently, traffic on the roads is growing at 7-10 per cent per annum. The share of roads in total traffic has been growing from 12 per cent of freight traffic and 31.6 percent passenger traffic in 1950-51 to a projected 65 per cent of freight traffic and 87 per cent of passenger traffic by the end of the Tenth Plan period. The rapid expansion and strengthening of the road network, therefore, is an imperative, both to provide for present and future traffic and for improved accessibility to the hinterland. In addition, road transport needs to be regulated for better energy efficiency, lesser pollution and enhanced road safety.

CHART 10.1

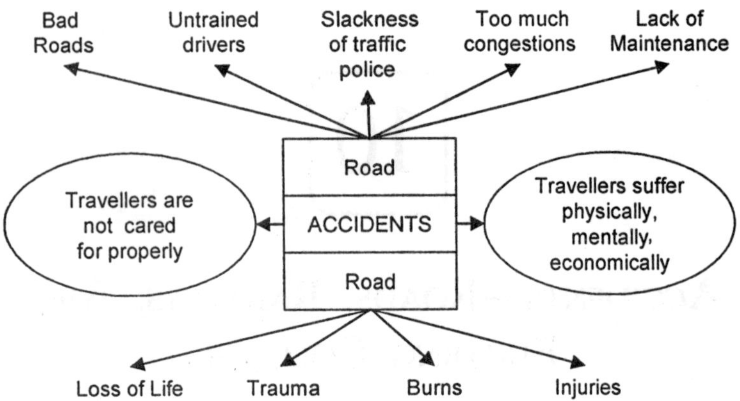

All this requires a massive infusion of funds. Historically, investments in roads, especially highways, was done by the government mainly because of the large volume of resources required, long gestation period of projects, 'uncertain returns. and various associated externalities. In recent times, the massive and ever increasing resource requirements and the concern for managerial efficiency and consumer responsiveness have led to the private sector being actively involved in the development and maintenance of the National Highways. The Ministry has formulated comprehensive policy guidelines to encourage private sector participation in the highway sector, besides providing several incentives such as tax exemptions and duty-free import of road building equipment and machinery. Model Concession Agreements have also been finalized for major road projects.[1]

The traffic accident has come to be considered as among the deadliest of killer diseases. This disease is a problem that the motor age has created and we are sluggish in our attitude to adapt ourselves to the hazards of the motor vehicle as compared to our concern and adaptability to the maladies attached to other killer diseases.

ROAD TRAFFIC HAZARDS: HIDDEN EPIDEMICS

More than 20 million people are severely injured or killed on the world's roads each year. The burden falls most heavily on developing countries, where it will grow heavier still because of the rapid increase in the number of vehicles.

In addition to the direct costs of road injuries and deaths, the increase in the number of vehicles' and reliance on certain transport policies have other serious health implications as well as wider social, economic and environmental impacts.[2] In some countries, air pollution from road transport causes even more deaths than those resulting from traffic accidents.[3] Besides the direct impacts on respiratory and heart disease, motorized transport produces around a quarter of the anthropogenic emissions of gases leading to climate change.[4] These "hidden epidemics" receive relatively little national or international attention compared with the focus on major communicable and non-communicable diseases.

To a large extent, road injuries are preventable. There are available and affordable interventions that can prevent injuries and save lives: to date, most of the evaluation of these interventions has been carried out in developed countries, and more research is needed on their effectiveness in developing countries. Renewed efforts are under way to increase worldwide awareness of the problem and its solutions and to encourage the introduction of road safety policies and practices. Several countries are using integrated strategies to deal with traffic risks and enhance the benefits of transport and land-use policies to promote physical activity and cohesive projects for community development.[5]

In addition to the unacceptable human toll, the global economic cost of road crashes has been estimated at about US $ 518 billion annually, of which the developing country share is about US $ 65 billion.[6] Countries struggling for economic development clearly cannot afford such losses, which have a significant impact on national health care systems. Injuries account for approximately one-third of the acute patient load in many hospitals in low-income and middle-income countries, and between 30% and 86% of all trauma admissions[7] road traffic injuries constitute the majority of such admissions.

Although more than 3000 people are killed each day, full recognition of the scale of the problem is obscured because road crashes usually cause only a few deaths at a time and generate little press coverage, contributing to the hidden nature of the epidemic of road traffic injuries.[8]

The problem of traffic accidents is more acute in developing countries. Thus in respect of safety on roads, our own country's position is far from satisfactory. More than 60,000 human lives are lost in road accidents each year. In a study conducted in 1990 for the Planning Commission, the economic cost of a fatal accident has been placed at Rs. 2 lakh, that of an injury accident at Rs. 1 lakh and the average cost of a minor non-injury accident, at Rs. 3,000. This should give us an idea of what kind of economic loss we are confronted with on account of road accidents each year.

Trend of Accidents in our Country

There is no denying the fact that the number of road accidents is high. However, the rate of road accidents per ten thousand vehicles has been coming down, as can be seen in Table 10.1.

Road Accidents Scenario

More than Eighty Thousand people are killed and around four lakh injured in about four lakh reported road accidents in the country every year. The following tables show the number of accidents, persons killed and injured in the country on all roads during 1997 to 2002. (Tables 10.2 and 10.3)

Cost of Accidents

A Working Group set-up by the Planning Commission in the year 2000 under the Chairmanship of Shri Prakash Narain, Former Chairman, Railway Board and Former Secretary, Shipping & Transport to look into road accidents, injury, prevention and control had gone into the issue of social cost of accidents in our country we had estimated the

TABLE 10.1

Number of Road Accidents and Deaths per 10,000 Vehicles

Year	*Number of road accidents per 10,000 vehicles*	*Number of persons killed per 10,000 vehicles*
1970	814.42	103.50
1980	338.86	54.41
1990	147.55	28.25
1998	90.07	19.32
1999	86.12	18.27
2000	80.89	16.31
2001	73.76	14.70
2002 (P)	68.32	14.05

(P) = Provisional.
Source: Ministry of Road Transport and Highway.

TABLE 10.2

No. of Accidents and Persons Killed/Injured

Year	*No. of Accidents*	*Persons killed*	*Persons injured*
1997	373671	76977	378361
1998	385018	79919	390674
1999	386456	81966	375051
2000	391449	78911	399265
2001	405637	80888	403751
2002	402157	82717	404829

Source: Ministry of Road Transport and Highway.

TABLE 10.3

Number of Persons Killed/Injured on National Highways

Year	*No. of Accidents*	*Persons killed*	*Persons injured*
1997	94014	25863	87375
1998	98690	26682	94175
1999	103839	28713	98427
2000	110508	30216	124600
2001	115824	32108	119592
2002	128632	32563	129966

(P) = Provisional
Source: Ministry of Road Transport and Highway.

cost at Rs. 55,000 crores in the year 1999-2000, which constituted 3% of the GDP for the year.

Reasons for Road Accidents

An analysis of accidents data shows that the primary causes of road accidents are driver's fault (83.5%), pedestrian fault/fault of passengers (4.7%), mechanical defect in vehicles (3%), bad roads (1.1%), bad weather (0.9%) and other factors like cattle, fallen blockage, road blockage, non-functioning of signals, absence of rear reflectors/road signages, etc. (6.8%).

National Road Safety Policy

The trend of increase in the vehicle population in the country is as in Table 10.4.

It may be seen that the vehicle population has been

TABLE 10.4

Increase in Vehicles Population

Year	*1951*	*1961*	*1971*	*1981*	*1991*	*1996*	*2000*	*2001*	*2002*	*2003*
No. of Vehicles	306	665	1865	5391	21374	33786	48857	54991	58863	64804(P)

E = Estimate.
Source: Ministry of Road Transport and Highway.

steadily increasing with the trend picking up significantly since the Eighties. Increase in vehicle population in the face of the limited road space which incidentally is used by a large variety of motorized and non-motorized traffic, has led the Government to accord a high priority to road safety. A draft Road Safety Policy was therefore prepared by the Ministry in the year 1992.

According to the available records, the draft Policy was discussed and adopted on 22.12.1994 in the fourth meeting of the National Road Safety Council, an apex level body constituted in the year 1987. A copy of the National Road Safety Policy adopted is at Annexure II. The policy document contained the following salient points:

- Classification of the cause of accident and

preventive action in terms of vehicle, driver, and engineering factors;

- List of safety features of vehicle design (e.g. safety belt, air bags, collapsible stirrings, braking performance, etc.);
- Fitness certification and maintenance of vehicles;
- Proper training and effective licensing for drivers;
- Road design and geometric improvements to compensate for inadequacies of road users;
- Warning signs for road users;
- Accidents, black spot investigation and rectification through road design;
- Design of road junctions;
- Design of roads in built up and residential areas, etc.;
- Traffic guidance, road signs, speed limit posts, and other traffic control devices;
- Road pavement markings, construction of footpaths/cycle tracks, bus bays, truck parking complexes, and other way side amenities, etc.;
- Traffic education and campaign on traffic discipline-inclusion of traffic education in school curriculum, promotion of defensive driving, etc.;
- Enforcement of maximum speed limits, and campaign on helmet use and seat belt use, curbing alcohol consumption among drivers, etc.; and
- Emergency medical service with emphasis on saving the lives of victims, etc.

Causes of Road Accidents

Various reasons for road accidents in India are: Lack of Traffic discipline on the part of drivers and road users, phenomenal increase in the number of motor vehicles with non-corresponding increase in road capacity, mixed traffic conditions, over-speeding, overloading, drunken driving, mechanical defects in vehicles, etc. The main causes of road accidents as revealed by the accident statistics in order of decreasing severity are as in Table 10.5.

TABLE 10.5

Reasons for Road Accidents

	Reasons for Road Accidents	*Percentage*
(a)	Fault of drivers	83.5
(b)	Mechanical defects of vehicles	3.0
(c)	Fault of pedestrians	2.3
(d)	Fault of passengers	2.4
(e)	Bad road	1.1
(f)	Bad weather	0.9
(g)	Other causes (cattles, fallen trees, Road Blockage, Sudden failure of the vehicles ahead, Absence of Rear Reflectors, Non-functioning of Signals and Absence of Road Signages, etc.	6.8
	Totals	100

Source: Report of Working Group for Tenth Five Year Plan.

CONCLUSION

The vast number of those maimed and killed on the roads are too often accepted fatalistically as a normal part of modern life. Yet, if traffic accidents are tackled by methods like those used against the great killing diseases, the present epidemic of road deaths can be made to diminish just as epidemics of plague and smallpox have now been almost completely eliminated every where in the world.

Some of the important steps being taken by the Government besides highway design to check the road accidents in the countries are as under:

(1) Assistance for setting up of Driving Training Schools.
(2) Provision of refresher training to drivers of heavy motor vehicles.
(3) Publicity campaign on road awareness through audio-visual print media.
(4) Grants-in-aid to voluntary organizations for administering road safety programme.

(5) Encouraging use of simulators in driver's training.
(6) Institution of National Award for voluntary organizations/individuals for outstanding work in the field of road safety.
(7) Organizing All India Essay Competition on road safety for school children with a view to create awareness.
(8) Tightening of fitness norms of transport vehicles. Widening/improvements of roads, etc.

RAILWAY ACCIDENTS

Safety

Railway accidents are one of the worst kind of disasters which result in loss of human lives and public property. They also lead to the entire railway operations being thrown out of tune and thus giving rise to a lot of public misery and outcry. Besides causing enormous national loss both direct and indirect, they also tarnish the image of the Indian Railways (IR). The hindrances to smooth flow of traffic which are caused as a result of accidents, become a big drain on several related aspects like coal movement, power generation and consequent snowballing effect on other sectors of economy.

The corporate mission of Indian Railways is "to be a modern railway system with sufficient capacity to meet the country's transport needs, both for passenger and freight traffic based on an optimal inter-modal mix and to provide this transportation at least cost to the society while maintaining financial viability of the system". The motto of the Indian Railways is "Safety, Security and Punctuality". An efficient and reliable transport system must necessarily be a safe and secure system. The corporate mission and motto are thus both clear indicators that the Indian Railways have recorded the highest priority to Safety.

"Railway Minister in his Budget Speech 2007-08 remarked Railway safety is our prime concern. I am glad to inform the House that funds for replacement of overaged Railway assets are now provided as soon as the assets become due for replacement. Sir, we have allocated Rs. 5,500 crore towards Depreciation Reserve Fund for the year 2007-08 as compared to Rs. 2,100 crore provided in 2001-02. This has had a direct impact on Railways' safety record. Although the gross traffic volume has increased from 724 Million train kilometers in 2001-02 to 825 Million train kilometers in 2005-06, the number of accidents is expected to be less than 200 in 2006-07 against 473 in the year 2001.

Of the Rs. 17,000 crore Special Railway Safety Fund, most of the works of renewal of overaged tracks, bridges, track circuiting and rolling stock will be completed by March 2007 and all remaining works will be completed by March 2008. Sir, as per our Corporate Safety Plan, the testing of Anti-Collision Device on North East Frontier Railway is in its last phase and is likely to be completed by March 2007. Besides this, The General Managers of the Zonal Railways have been delegated the powers to approve construction of subways costing upto Rs. 50 lacs, to reduce accidents at unmanned level crossings. The production of batter crash worthy coaches has commanded. In future, the number of such coaches will be further increased to ensure safety of passengers.

IR is quite unique and distinctive in character, really a microcosm of India. To make it a safe and reliable system is an enormous challenge. The Railways has the most intricate and involved interdependencies. Safety on the Railways is the end product of the cohesive fusion of its myriad parts. A single flaw in the 63,332 route kms of track that crises—cross the country, a defect in the 8000 locos, 44,000 coaches and 2.1 lakh wagons that haul more than 15 million passengers and around 2 million tons of freight every day, an incorrect indication of one of the thousands of signals that dot the rail landscape, a mistake or an act of negligence by one of its 6,00,000 frontline staff directly associated with train running, even a rash act by one of the millions of road users who daily negotiate the 34,000 odd level crossing gates spread across the system, an irresponsible act of carrying inflammable goods—any one of these multiple possibilities has the potential to cause a major tragedy. Added to these are the acts of sabotage by misguided elements spanning the whole country. Thus utmost vigil in safety in operations and also security of the traveling public is accorded by the Railways. To address to the ever growing need for safety, Railways have had constituted various committees over the augmenting the same. The last committee Railway Safety Review Committee (RSRC) was constituted in 1997 under the chairmanship of Justice H.C. Khanna which had given various grant of Rs. 15,000 crore to the Railways to enable it to clear its arrears of replacement and renewals in a fixed time schedule. Based on this recommendation, the Government had set-up a non-lapsable Special Railway Safety Fund in the year 2001-02 for completing the task in period of five to six years, i.e. upto 2006-07. The fund was to receive an amount of Rs. 17,000 cr over the period. Almost 90% of the works have been completed and for the balance 10%, which are spilling over to 2007-08 due to delays in contractual obligations and non-availability of critical inputs, the Railways are being allowed to extend the validity of operating this fund by another one year.

Accident Related Data

As a result of various safety measures and sustained efforts over the years there has been a declining trend in the number of consequential train accidents, which has come down from 473 in 2000-01 to 415 in 2001-02, 351 in 2002-03 and 325 in 2003-04 and further to 234 in 2005-06.

Another important index of train safety, viz., number of consequential train accidents per million train kms has come down consistently from 0.65 during 2000-01 to 0.28 during 2005-06, which is the lowest achieved so far, despite quantum jump in the volumes of traffic being carried by the Indian Railways over the years. (See Table 10.6)

Organisation for Railway Safety

The Commission of Railway Safety functions independent of the Ministry of Railway under the administrative control of the Ministry of Civil Aviation and deals with matters pertaining to Safety of rail travel and train operation and is charged with certain regulatory, inspectorial, investigatory and advisory functions as laid down in the Railway Act, 1989. The Commission is headed by a Chief

TABLE 10.6

Consequential Train Accidents since 2000-01

Type of Accident	*2000–01*	*2001-02*	*2002-03*	*2003-04*	*2004-05*	*2005-06 upto Jan.*	*2005-06 upto Jan.*	*2006-07*
Collision	20	30	16	9	13	9	9	8
	4.23%	7.23%	4.56%	2.77%	5.56%	3.85%	4.46%	4.65%
Derailments	350	280	218	202	138	131	109	82
	74.00%	67.47%	62.11%	62.15%	58.97%	55.98%	53.96%	47.67%
Manned level crossing gate accidents	11	8	14	9	5	10	8	7
	2.33%	1.93%	3.99%	2.77%	2.14%	4.27%	3.96%	4.07%
Unmanned level crossing accidents	73	80	82	86	65	65	59	64
	15.43%	19.28%	23.36%	26.46%	27.78%	27.78%	29.21%	37.21%
Fire in train	17	9	14	14	10	15	14	4
	3.59%	2.17%	3.99%	4.31%	4.27%	6.41%	6.93%	2.33%
Miscellaneous	2	8	7	5	3	4	3	7
	0.42%	1.93%	1.99%	1.54%	1.28%	1.71%	1.49%	4.07%
Total	473	415	351	325	234	234	202	172
Accident per million train kilometers	0.65	0.55	0.44	0.41	0.29	0.28		

Source: Ministry of Railway, 2006-07.

Commissioner of Railway Safety at Lucknow. Working under the administrative control of the Chief Commissioner of Railway Safety are 10 Commissioners of Railway Safety, each one exercising Jurisdiction over one of the 9 zonal Railways and the Metro Railway.

The principal functions of the Commission of Railway Safety are:

(i) Inspection of new Railway lines prior to authorisation for passenger traffic.
(ii) Periodical inspection of open lines;
(iii) Approval of new works and renewals affecting passenger carrying trains;
(iv) Investigations into accidents, including enquiries into such accidents to passenger carrying trains as are considered to be of a serious nature; and
(v) General advice on matters concerning safety in train operations.

Section 113 of Railway Act, 1989 requires intimation o serious accidents to be sent to the Commissioner of Railway Safety. Under the Statutory Investigation into Accidents Rules, 1998 framed by the Ministry of Civil Aviation and Tourism, a Statutory enquiry by the Commissioner of Railway Safety is obligatory in every serious accidents to a train carrying passengers which is attended with loss of human life, or with grievous hurt, as defined in the Indian Penal Code, to or with grievous hurt, as defined in the Indian Penal Code, to a passenger or passengers in the train or with serious damage to railway property of the value exceeding Rs. 25 lakhs. While holding statutory enquiry, the Commission not only examines affected passengers but also invites members of the public to given evidence in persons during the enquiry or to write to the Commission. Some of the serious accidents at manned level crossings attended with loss of life or with grievous injury to persons traveling in road vehicles are also inquired into by the Commission of Railway Safety. The Commissioner of Railway Safety stops or discontinues his enquiry whenever the Central Government appoints a Commission of Inquiry under the Commission of Inquiries Act, 1952.

The Commission, in its discretion, may hold enquiry into any other accident.

The commission of Railway Safety should be placed in the Ministry of Railways, on the lines of Director General of Civil Aviation, who continues to be part of the Ministry of Civil Aviation, while performing safety functions including accident inquiries, by amending relevant portions of Railways Act, 1989 and "allocation of business rules" accordingly. There can be a distinct and strengthened organization within the Ministry of Railways, which can still function independently (Its status may be similar as that of Railway Claims Tribunal or Railways Rates Tribunal). The Commission can be made multi-disciplinary by inducting not only senior officers of five major departments of the Railways, but also, experts from the field of forensic science, security and law and order enforcement agencies. This will dispel the general perception that the existing structure of the commission is amendable to influence owing to its perceived habitual allegiance to Railways.

OR

- Continuance of the present system with recruitment base being expanded, as recommended by RSRC, by opening it to the five major departments of the Railways.

OR

- Continuance of the present system with the recruitment base remaining the same and remaining under the Ministry of Civil Aviation.

Railways are making efforts to sustain this declining trend during the current year also, except in case of accidents at unmanned level crossings, mainly caused due to failure of road users; a reduction is seen in case of every other category of accident as is evident from the Table 10.7.[9]

Let us analyse the causes of railway accidents as mentioned in Table 10.7.

TABLE 10.7

Cause-wise Analysis of Accidents since 2000-01

Causes	*2000-01*	*2001-02*	*2002-03*	*2003-04*	*2004-05*	*2005-06*	*2005-06 upto Jan.*	*2006-07 upto Jan.*
Failure of Railway Staff	293 61.95%	248 59.76%	186 52.99%	161 49.54%	119 50.85%	120 51.28%	100 49.50%	79 45.93%
Failure of other than Railway Staff	109 23.04%	103 24.82%	118 33.62%	107 32.92%	78 33.33%	86 36.75%	78 38.61%	73 42.44%
Failure of equipment	33 6.98%	24 5.78%	18 5.13%	18 5.54%	14 5.98%	8 3.42%	7 3.47%	3 1.74%
Sabotage	19 4.02%	14 3.37%	10 2.85%	18 5.54%	4 1.71%	5 2.14%	5 1.98%	8 4.65%
Combination of factors	4 0.85%	—	2 0.57%	2 0.62%	1 0.43%	—	—	—
Incidental	11 2.33%	20 4.82%	15 4.27%	17 5.23%	16 —	11 4.70%	9 4.46%	7 4.07%
Could not be established conclusively	4 0.85%	5 1.20%	2 0.57%	2 0.62%	2 0.85%	3 1.28%	3 1.49%	—
Under investigation	—	1 0.24%	—	—	—	1 0.43%	1 0.50%	2 1.16%
Grand total	473	415	351	325	234	234	202	172

Source: Ibid.

1. Collision Most Dreaded Accident

Collisions are the most dreaded accidents for any railway-man. These can be 'side collisions', 'Rear-end' and 'head-on collisions'. Trains ramming into another from behind are called rear-end collisions, while trains colliding on the same track from opposite ends, are called head-on collisions and are the most fatal of all accidents. Side collisions can occur either in station areas, while converging or diverging or by fouling the adjacent track in multiple line territory. Rear-end collisions and head-on collisions can occur at stations or between the stations.

2. Manned Level Gate Crossing Accidents

Despite gradual manning of level crossings, construction of Road overbridges/Road underbridges (ROBs/RUBs) and intensive public awareness campaigns, it has not been possible for the Indian Railways to tackle the problem of reduction of level crossing accidents. As they are predominantly due to lapses on the part of road users, and in view of stupendous increase in road traffic, there does not appear to be any let up in the mishaps. As the IR do not have much direct physical control or intervention, it will be the aim of the Indian Railways, at least, to contain and control the accidents at rail-road intersections at the existing level. A coordinated approach, involving State Governments., various influence-groups and intensive social awareness programmes will be principal measures to attain the objective.

3. Derailments

The derailments, being the largest component of total consequential train accidents is required to be tackled with greater urgency. Around 75% of derailments occur due to 'railway staff failure', and another 10% derailments are caused by 'equipment failures'. Around 15% are caused by failure of 'other than railway staff', sabotage and incidental reasons.

4. Fire Accidents

Though the average number of fire accidents as well as

the annual average fatalities are 8 per year for both, a stray major fire in train accident may lead to disaster. In general, nearly 40% of fire accidents are caused by unidentified elements, on which the Railways have little control. With the rising social awareness, stringent scrutiny on trains, induction of fire-proof coaches and more and more technological inputs, it is assessed that the fire accidents and consequent fatalities would be reduced by 80% as compared to their present level.

Objectives of the Safety

The goals to be achieved to enhance safety on Indian Railways are:

- To make railways more reliable and a safer mode for transportation of men and material.
- To stimulate the implementation of modern, proactive and systematic safety measures.
- To bring about both qualitative and quantitative improvements in safety performance.
- To encourage safety research and development.
- To reduce consequential train accidents.

Need for Safety Culture

Safety is an ethos that should pervade all activities of railway operations and maintenance. This ethos has to be installed and nurtured. It is not an attribute that is likely to be evident merely because rules are reiterated or instructions issued. The concern for safety has to be all pervasive in the functioning of the Indian Railways.[10]

In addition, there are accidents occurring in the Air as the Air Travel is increasing fast. We must attend to it regularly.

Besides, in recent years there are disasters due to stample and collapse of buildings. Only in 2008 (Sept. 2008) 250 people died in Chamunda Devi in Jodhpur (Rajasthan) in Naina Devi (Himachal Pradesh) about 200 people die due to stampede and building collapse. We must learn the art and science of managing crowds attending public functions and remove those buildings, bridges which have become dangerous.

Recently, bad elements in a society are creating fear among people through their anti-social people through their anti-social activities like planting of bombs, dacoity, rape, killing people. These need be curbed to promote peace otherwise life would become hell as in minds of people, the fear would be lurking causing damage to devélopment, harmony, peace and goodwill.

CONCLUSION

Safety of life of people is most essential for any government. Though the duties of government have increase, but they have to cope with it as it falls into essential duties. People must also co-operate. There is a need of training to both entrusted with law and orders as well as the people. Mutual cooperation would reduce the chances of accidents.

Notes and References

1. Annual Report, 2003-04, M/o Road Transport and Highways, GOI, New Delhi, p. 5.
2. Dora, C., Phillips, M., Transport Environment and Health, Copenhagen, World Health Organization, Regional Office for Europe, 2000, (WHO Regional Publication, European Series, No. 89.
3. Kunzil, N., *et. al.*, Public Health impact of outdoor and traffic-related in air pollution; a European assessment, Lancet, 2000, 356-795, 801.
4. Metz, B. *et al.*, Climate Change, 2001, Mitigation, Cambridge, Cambidge University Press for the Inter-Governmental Panel on Climate Change (IPCC), 2001.
5. Dora, C., Racioppi, F., Including health in transport policy agencies, the role of health impact assessment analysis and procedures in the European experience, *Bulletin of the World Health Organization*, 2003, 81; 399-404.
6. Jacobs, G., Aaron-Thomas, A., Astrop, A., Estimating global road fatalities, London, Transport Research Laboratory, 2000 (TRL, Report No. 445).
7. Odero, W., Garner, P., Zwi, A., Road Traffic injuries in development countries, a comprehensive revive of epidemiological studies, *Tropical Medicine and International Health*, 1997, 2; 445-60.
8. WHO; The World Health Report, 2003, Geneva, pp. 95-96.
9. *Ibid.*, p. 29.
10. GOI, Ministry of Railways, Corporate Safety Plan, 2003-12, pp. 4-5.

APPENDIX 10.1

Total Number of Accidents on all Roads and National Highways

Sl. No.	States/UTs	Total No. of Accidents			Accidents on N.H.		
		2000	2001	2002 (P)	2000	2001	2002 (R)
1.	Andhra Pradesh	25398	30031	27634	7203	9096	8185
2.	Arunachal Pradesh	252	264	244	70	93	78
3.	Assam	2492	2516	2625	1889	1927	1928
4.	Bihar	4397	2873	N.A	2127	1167	Na
5.	Chhattisgarh	6913	8751	8664	2096	2597	5531
6.	Goa	2961	2818	3419	1091	1184	1404
7.	Gujarat	36029	32523	31735	8113	67387	7239
8.	Haryana	8206	8393	8748	2765	3033	2315
9.	Himachal Pradesh	2039	2371	2542	709	898	1047
10.	Jammu and Kashmir	4598	4610	5394	2328	536	2141
11.	Jharkhand	3763	4028	4711	1409	1392	1817
12.	Karnataka	32397	33000	35784	9605	9906	10246
13.	Kerala	37072	38361	38762	8512	10095	10840
14.	Madhya Pradesh	23805	26239	26929	5611	6136	7347
15.	Maharashtra	71550	74521	66876	16050	14576	13417
16.	Manipur	506	409	520	217	208	263
17.	Meghalaya	392	600	172	186	370	113
18.	Mizoram	72	83	96	31	52	54
18.	Nagaland	79	102	84	35	54	29
29.	Orissa	6611	6405	6848	2784	3940	2920
21.	Punjab	3876	4171	4692	1298	1329	1588
22.	Rajasthan	19932	19999	20571	6718	7465	7214
23.	Sikkim	94	109	228	29	43	109
24.	Tamil Nadu	48923	51978	35503	18615	19881	22091
25.	Tripura	524	544	624	184	230	164
26.	Uttaranchal	877	1060	1117	236	469	542
27.	Uttar Pradesh	16644	20474	20684	6198	8914	7849
28.	West Bengal	18989	16954	17974	2443	3795	10002
U.Ts							
1.	Andaman and Nicobar	158	181	168	0	0	0
2.	Chandigarh	455	492	494	62	45	99
3.	Dadra and Nagar Haveli	84	88	80	0	0	0
4.	Daman and Diu	66	53	69	0	0	0
5.	Delhi	10245	9344	8699	1277	1123	1030
6.	Lakshadweep	6	6	3	0	0	0
7.	Pondicherry	1054	1286	1484	537	595	730
	TOTAL	391449	405637	402158	110508	115824	128632

Appendix I

DIASTER ADMINISTRATION

DISASTER MANAGEMENT

Overview

Many regions in India are highly vulnerable to natural and other disasters on account of geological conditions. About 60% of the landmass is susceptible to earthquakes and over 8% is prone to floods. Of the nearly 7500 kilometers long coastline, approximately 5700 kilometers is prone to cyclones. 68% area is susceptible to drought. All this entails huge economic losses and causes developmental setbacks. Disasters are no longer limited to natural catastrophes. Man-made emergencies often cause bigger disasters in terms of fatalities and economic losses. With urbanization and concentration of population in metropolitan cities, more and more people are becoming vulnerable to locational disasters. So, the development process needs to be sensitive towards disaster prevention, preparedness and mitigation. Disaster management has therefore emerged as a high priority for the country. Going beyond the historical focus on relief and rehabilitation after the event, there is a need to look ahead and plan for disaster preparedness and mitigation in order to ensure that periodic shocks to our development efforts are minimized.

Disaster risk reduction has not been highlighted in the policies and programmes of various plan schemes. The country's commitment to mainstreaming disaster risk reduction into the process of development planning at all levels so as to achieve sustainable development is yet to be carried forward across sectors through actionable programmes for achieving the desired result.

Tenth Five Year Plan Strategy and Approach

The Tenth Five Year Plan (2002-07), prepared in the

Source: GOI, Planning Commission, Eleventh Five Year Plan, 2007-12, Vol. I, pp. 207-22.

backdrop of the Orissa super cyclone, Gujarat earthquake, and end of the International Decade of Natural Disaster Reduction, recognized disaster management as a development issue for the first time. The Plan devoted a separate chapter to disaster management and made a number of important prescriptions to mainstream disaster risk reduction into the process of development.

The Tenth Plan prescriptions on disaster management can broadly be divided into three categories:

(i) Policy guidelines at the macro-level that would inform and guide the preparation and implementation of development plans across sectors;
(ii) Operational guidelines for integrating disaster management practices into development plans and programmes; and
(iii) Specific developmental schemes for prevention and mitigation of disasters.

At the macro-level, the Plan emphasized that 'while hazards, both natural or otherwise, are inevitable, the disasters that follow need not be so and the society can be prepared to cope with them effectively whenever they occur' and called for a 'multi-pronged strategy for total risk management, comprising prevention, preparedness, response and recovery, on the one hand, and for initiating development efforts aimed towards risk reduction and mitigation, on the other. It stated that only then could we look forward development'.

At the operational level, the Plan made a number of very important suggestions, as given below:

- Streamlining institutional arrangements for disaster response by an integrated approach involving civilian and military resources; setting up a modern, permanent national command centre or operations room with redundant communications and data links to all State capitals; establishing a quick response team particularly for search and rescue operations; developing standard operating system for dealing with humanitarian and relief assistance from non-government sources; and formulating a unified legislation for dealing with all types of disasters.

- Building disaster prevention and preparedness in development planning by introducing a rigorous process of vulnerability analysis and risk assessment, maintaining comprehensive database and resource inventories at all levels, developing state-of-the-art infrastructure for mitigation planning, and establishing a Disaster Knowledge Network for the use of disaster managers, decision-makers, community, and so on.
- Developing a nation-wide culture of prevention by introducing disaster management in the school curriculum, including relevant aspects of disaster management in professional courses, enhancing the capacity of disaster managers by better training facilities and creating a massive awareness at all levels. Encouraging community level initiatives for disaster preparedness by involving people at the grass-roots, particularly those who are more vulnerable, for better preparedness and response.
- Developing appropriate zonal regulations, design standards, building codes, and performance specifications for safe construction.
- Inclusion of disaster mitigation analysis in all development schemes in vulnerable areas through which the feasibility of a project is assessed with respect to vulnerability of the area.
- Building disaster mitigation components into all development projects financed under the Plan.

The Tenth Plan felt that planned expenditure on disaster mitigation and prevention measures was required in addition to a Calamity Relief Fund. The Plan, however, stopped short of recommending any specific plan scheme for prevention, mitigation or preparedness for disasters nor did it allocate any amount for such scheme, except making a general recommendation that 'Creation of faculties in disaster management in all 28 states is proposed to be taken up in the Tenth Plan in addition to community mobilization, human resource development, establishment of Control Rooms and forging international cooperation in disaster management. There is also an urgent need for strengthening the disaster management pedagogy by creating disaster management faculties in universities, rural development institutes and other organizations of premier research.'

Implementation of Schemes in the Tenth Plan

A Central Sector Plan Scheme, the National Disaster Mitigation Programme (NDMP), has been implemented since 1993-94. The scheme mainly provided for training and capacity building of government functionaries and other stakeholders to manage disasters in an effective manner. This scheme was transferred from the Ministry of Agriculture to the Ministry of Home Affairs in June 2002. The allocation for this scheme was raised from Rs. 6.30 crore in the Eighth Plan to Rs. 16.32 crore in the Ninth Plan and to Rs. 30.77 crore in Tenth Plan. The annual allocations under various components of the scheme during the Tenth Five Year Plan are in Table 1.

Out of the eight components of the above scheme, only two components namely 'Grants-in-Aid' and 'Professional Services' were developmental in nature, while the remaining components were on revenue expenses. The major activities under the grants-in-aid include the setting up of the National Centre for Disaster Management at the Indian Institute of Public Administration, now upgraded as a statutory organization known as National Institute of Disaster Management (NIDM), creation of 29 disaster management faculties/Centres in 28 States, research and consultancy services, and documentation of major disaster events. The faculties did not have sufficient back-up from the States with the result that only limited activities are undertaken by the Centres. Even meagre allocations provided by the Central Government as grants-in-aid were not fully utilized in many of the States. The allocation of Rs. 21.90 crore to the training

TABLE I

National Disaster Mitigation Programme-Year-wise Allocation of Funds in the Tenth Five Year Plan

(Rs. in lakh)

S. No.	*Head*	*2002-03*	*2003-04*	*2004-05*	*2005-06*	*2006-07*	*Total*
1	.Grants-in-aid	262.00	349.00	474.00	505.00	600.00	2190.00
2.	Professional Services	20.00	29.00	54.00	110.00	150.00	363.00
3.	Machinery & Equipments	2.00	20.00	30.00	15.00	10.00	77.00
4.	Foreign Travel	80.00	30.00	25.00	40.00	50.00	225.00
5.	Contribution	20.00	20.00	20.00	17.00	20.00	97.00
6.	Office Expenses	2.50	3.00	2.00	2.00	2.00	11.50
7.	Advertisement & Publicity	20.00	10.00	25.00	1.00	1.00	57.00
8.	Other Charges	0.50	26.00	10.00	10.00	10.00	56.50
	Total	407.00	487.00	640.00	700.00	843.00	3077.00

Source: Disaster Management Division (MHA).

institutes during the Tenth Five Year Plan was mainly used on NIDM which incurred an expenditure of Rs. 11.56 crore. Nearly 71,000 persons have been imparted training under the programme (Table 1).

The National Cyclone Risk Mitigation Project is another Plan Scheme proposed to be implemented with World Bank assistance. The project is presently at the stage of preparation of Detailed Project Report. It covers all 13 cyclone prone coastal States and UTs. Investments are to be made in upgradation of cyclone forecasting, tracking and warning systems, construction work of cyclone shelters, road linkages, plantation, retro-fittings of vital lifeline installations, strengthening of national and regional training institutions, setting up a technological regime for cyclone mitigation and for strong management and monitoring system. As regards upgradation of cyclone forecasting, tracking and warning systems, this activity is proposed to be taken up either as part of the project or independently by the IMD.

The Ministry of Home Affairs is also implementing Phase II of a Community-based Disaster Risk Mitigation (DRM) Programme in 169 multi-hazard districts in 17 States/ UTs with the support of UNDP under a multi-donor programme at a total estimated cost of Rs. 153 crore (US$34 million). Under this programme, disaster management plans are being prepared from village to district; village volunteers are being trained in first-aid, search and rescue, evacuation and relief and shelter management; disaster management teams are being constituted at the district and sub-district levels and mock drills are being conducted at all levels. This 100% externally funded programme is, however, outside the framework of the Plan and is being implemented on the non-Plan side. It is the largest community-based DRM programme in the world. Phase I of the programme was implemented in the three States of Gujarat, Orissa, and Bihar during 2002-06 and has been rated well in a recent evaluation conducted by a team of consultants. While the general feedback on Phase II of the programme is good, there is a definite need to increase the scope to cover other deficient areas too, in order to draw the full benefit from this.

INSTITUTIONAL AND OTHER INITIATVES IN THE TENTH PLAN

The following significant initiatives on disaster management were taken during the Tenth Five Year Plan period:

- The Disaster Management Act, 2005 has been enacted for establishing requisite institutional mechanisms for drawing up and monitoring the implementation of disaster management plans, ensuring measures by various wings of the government for prevention and mitigating the effects of disasters, and for undertaking a holistic, co-ordinated, and prompt response to any disaster situation.
- The National Disaster Management Authority (NDMA), under the Chairmanship of the Prime Minister, has been set-up in terms of the Act. NDMA is an apex body responsible for laying down of policies, plans and guidelines on disaster management so as to ensure timely and effective response to disasters. The Authority has prepared a Draft National Policy on Disaster Management and has taken up preparation of guidelines on prevention, mitigation, response, and recovery in regard to various types of disasters such as earthquake, flood, landslides, industrial disaster, and so on. The guidelines on management of earthquake, chemical disasters, and chemical (industrial) disasters have been finalized and circulated.
- The State Governments are in the process of setting up State and district Disaster Management Authorities. The provisions of the Act relevant to the States/UTs have been brought into force w.e.f. 1 August 2007. While Arunachal Pradesh, Goa, Gujarat, Himachal Pradesh, Kerala, Mizoram, Puducherry, Punjab, and Uttar Pradesh are reported to have constituted SDMAs as per the Act, the other States/UTs are in the process of constituting the same.

- An eight battalion-strong National Disaster Response Force has been set-up comprising of 144 specialized response teams on various types of disasters of which 72 teams are for nuclear, biological, and chemical (NBC) disasters.
- The Civil Defence set-up in the country is proposed to be revamped to strengthen local efforts for disaster preparedness and effective response. Similarly, the Fire Services are also proposed to be strengthened/modernized to convert them into a multi-hazard response force.
- The National Institute of Disaster Management has been set-up for training, capacity building, research, and documentation on various natural and man-made disasters. A comprehensive Human Resource Plan for Disaster Management has also been developed.
- Disaster Management has been included in the curriculum of middle and secondary school education. The subject has also been included in the post-induction and in-service training of civil and police officers. Modules have also been identified to include disaster management aspects in the course curriculum for engineering, architecture, and medical degrees.
- A committee of experts has finalized the Model building by-laws for town and country planning legislations, land use zonaton, and development control legislations. The municipalities and city development authorities all over the country have been advised to make necessary changes in their respective by-laws and regulations in accordance with the model laws.
- The Bureau of Indian Standards has issued building codes for construction of different types of buildings in different seismic zones in the country. The National Building Code has also been revised, taking into consideration the natural hazards and risks of various regions of the country.

- The National Programme for Capacity Building of Engineers in Earthquake Risk Management to train 10,000 engineers and 10,000 architects on safe construction techniques and architectural practices is under implementation.
- A Web-enabled centralized inventory of resources has been developed to minimize response time in emergencies. Over 1,10,000 records from 600 districts have been uploaded.
- Safe construction practices and do's and don'ts for various hazards are being disseminated for creating public awareness.

Eleventh Plan

Vision and Strategy

The Tenth Plan has set into motion the process of shift in focus from response-centric disaster management covering rescue, relief, rehabilitation, and reconstruction to laying greater emphasis on the other elements of disaster management cycle-prevention, mitigation, and preparedness—as a means to avert or soften the impact of future emergencies. The Eleventh Plan aims at consolidating the process by giving impetus to projects and programmes that develop and nurture the culture of safety and the integration of disaster prevention and mitigation into the development process. The guidance and direction to achieve this paradigm shift will need to flow from NDMA, and in the true spirit of the Disaster Management Act, to all stakeholders including State Governments and UTs, right up to the PRIs. Communities at large will need to be mobilized to achieve this common objective as they are the first responders. Even the best of isolated efforts will not bear fruit unless they are part of an overall, well-considered approach, and responsibilities of all stakeholders are clearly spelt out and accountability and sustainability factored in.

Projects and programmes undertaken may be such that they address the felt national needs and with well acknowledged prioritization. With scarce resources, which will facilitate systematic project and programme appraisal.

Support will have to be lent to programmes and projects that will lead to sustainable development, with assurance of disaster risk reduction built in. The question of vulnerability will also have to be considered, not only in the physical sense but in a comprehensive sense; vulnerability could also be social, ecological, organizational, educational, attitudinal, political, cultural, and economical.

For an objective screening and scrutiny of development projects in a speedy manner, it is essential that professionalism in project formulation is insisted upon. Well-considered and well-drafted, need-based project proposals with in-built disaster prevention and mitigation features, as brought out above, should usually sail through the decision-making process. These projects would need to be based on sufficient studies, reliable assumptions, and have regard for the latest advances in science and technology.

To ensure thoroughness in project formulation, all the expected requirements need to be clearly articulated and the project appraisal procedure kept simple and straightforward. One set of standard guidelines may not be adequate in addressing all the complex set of issues and there is clearly a need to evolve a multi-pronged approach to address a host of interlinked issues.

For the assessment of impact of any major development scheme in a given zone of hazard, it is imperative that the proposal takes in its stride what all could go wrong (damage scenarios) and shows how the project design is fashioned to counter that likely damage scenario. Conceptualization of damage scenarios will require quality scientific studies in a multi-disciplinary environment, and generation of new data, besides filling data gaps.

The SoI needs to be entrusted with the responsibility of generating large-scale maps which will form the basis for disaster management studies. They will also need to generate a Digital Elevation Map (DEM) of high resolution (1/2m interval along vertical) for the purpose of 3D terrain modelling. There will be a need to carry out prioritization of the areas on which the SoI will carry out the 1:10000 mapping for the whole country and map all towns and cities on 1:2000 scales. Coastal zones and flood prone areas of the country will need to get priority in the preparation of DEM. NDMA, in consultation with National Informatics Centre (NIC), National Spatial Data Infrastructure, National Remote Sensing Agency, and DoS is actively promoting the use of GIS in all institutions concerned with disaster management. Priority will have to be given to highly vulnerable areas for generating the database for mapping as well as hazard vulnerability and risk assessment related to disasters like cyclone, flood earthquake, chemical and industrial, etc.

Data-sharing among the various data generators is an even more important aspect and needs to be addressed. All such schemes getting Plan funds will be treated as national asset and data would be made available without any pre-condition for use for disaster management authorities and others.

The national emergency communication network, involving the contemporary space and terrestrial-based technologies, in a highly synergistic configuration and with considerable redundancy, needs to be developed and deployed countrywide. With almost a 100% reliability, this network must ensure real-time dissemination of warnings and information direct to the affected community and local authorities.

Research on all aspects of disaster mitigation which has the potential to save lives and property needs to be encouraged. NDMA could provide the necessary policy direction to Science-related ministries and departments both at the Central and State levels to foster, promote, and sustain research and development work through need-based disaster mitigation and management projects.

A well sensitized and prepared community forms one of the most important links in the process of better management of disasters. For that reason, 'Extended Disaster Risk Mitigation Project' has been identified for being taken up for preparation of a Project Report during the Plan. This will be supplemented by activities under various other national/ State level mitigation projects. As far as Community Based Disaster Management is concerned, a degree of convergence is required to be brought into community mobilization, participation, awareness, and capacity building aspects of all concerned social sector schemes like women and child development, rural development, drinking water, sanitation, and so on. The concerned ministries may consider inclusion of disaster management content into their plans and make provision of funds in their respective schemes.

It is essential that while clearing plans for State Governments, there is an integrated approach, particularly for creation of adequate capacity for relief and rescue operations.

There is need for evolution of a broad classification of anticipated projects that would come up for clearance by the Planning Commission. One possible classification could be:

- Projects specifically designed in response to the NDMA Strategy, Guidelines and Action Plan, and
- Development projects with built-in environmental preservation and disaster mitigation features in tune with the philosophy of mainstreaming mitigation measures into development projects.

Assistance is needed for State level mitigation projects, especially drafting of State, district, and panchayat level disaster management plans and in continuous sustenance, modernization, and upgradation of disaster management capacity.

In view of the focus on disaster mitigation of projects, institution building, aimed at training a new breed of disaster managers, and establishment of centres/institutes fully equipped to carry out specialized investigations and post-disaster studies, would need to be encouraged. The training and skills of the 72 teams for NBC disasters in the eight Battalions of the National Disaster Response Force have to be improved and sharpened.

Out of the eight battalions of the National Disaster Response Force already sanctioned by the government, two Battalions already have the basic infrastructure. While the existing infrastructure has to be upgraded for these two Battalions, completely new infrastructure has to be created for the remaining six Battalions.

Mainstreaming Disaster Management into Development Planning

Mainstreaming disaster management into the development planning process essentially means looking critically at each activity that is being planned, no' only from the perspective of reducing the disaster vulnerability of that activity, but also from the perspective of minimizing that activity's potential contribution to the hazard. Every development plan of a ministry/department should incorporate elements of impact assessment, risk reduction, and the 'do no harm' approach. Examples of this approach are urban planning and zoning, upgradation of building codes and their effective enforcement, adoption of disaster resilient housing designs and construction of school and hospitals, flood proofing, response preparedness planning, insurance, establishment of early warning systems for various types of disasters, generating community awareness, creating technical competence and promoting research among engineers, architects, health experts, and scientists.

State governments need to give priority in their plans for schemes regarding hazard identification and risk assessment once they have prepared the project paper, completed preliminary work, and drawn up the details of the scheme. Hazard identification and risk assessment across the country must be bound by uniformly followed procedures, fine-tuned to local conditions. In the absence of such procedures, any sporadic activity based on some ad hoc procedure carries the potential of doing more harm than good. It will be essential that while clearing plans of State Governments, there is an integrated approach particularly for creation of adequate capacity for relief and rescue operations, for example, for funding projects for construction of school buildings. Some school buildings need to be identified which will be used as relief centres and buildings designed so that they withstand the impact of disasters and also have adequate capacity to provide space as relief centres. Such schools should be equipped with essential services which become important at the time of a disaster.

State governments will need to make comprehensive Management Action Plans for achieving long-term results in a phased manner. To make these plans more meaningful, workshops and training programmes are to be organized at local/regional/national levels for capacity building and awareness generation/community participation.

Outside the framework of Plan schemes, many innovative measures can be adopted to encourage disaster risk reduction measures by the corporate sector, non-government organizations, and individuals. Fiscal measures like rebates on income and property tax for retrofitting unsafe buildings, compulsory risk insurance for bank loan on all types of properties, and so on, shall definitely help to mobilize resources for safe construction and retrofitting of existing constructions in all disaster prone areas. Similarly, many innovative measures may be taken for promoting public-private-community partnership for disaster risk reduction.

Principles for Project Appraisal from the Disaster Management Perspective

To assist the Planning Commission in appraisal of projects, broad and generic guidelines which are not disaster or theme specific have to be adopted. Conceptualization of hazard scenarios and associated vulnerability and risk assessments in a given situation will necessarily have to depend on available maps, Master Plans and building and land use regulations, National Building Code of India, and the various safety Standards and Codes of the Bureau of Indian Standards. The guidelines will have to cover the following aspects:

- The location of the project is to be carefully considered, especially if this is in a multi-hazard prone area/district recognized by the NDMA. Multi-hazard prone districts are reported in the latest National Building Code of India of the Bureau of Indian Standards. The listing has been revised by the Building Materials Technology Promotion Council of India, currently under the consideration of NDMA

- The project/scheme should be based on a detailed hazard and risk assessment; wherever required, environmental clearance will also be taken. The risk assessment will usually involve the following factors:
  - o Assessment of degree of hazard, based on high resolution single/multiple hazard maps interpreted in the light of all available historic records, publications, site-specific information, and studies. For all major projects/schemes, where such maps are presently unavailable, the project/scheme should be supported by adequate site-specific seismo-tectonic, geological, geo-physical, and geotechnical studies and analyses. Data gaps, assumptions made, and their implications should be brought out. Where high resolution multi-hazard maps are not available, multi-hazard assessment is to be made by coalescing the information on single hazards.
  - o All such site specific risk assessment studies should be referenced to a national high resolution geospatial database so as to facilitate temporal analysis of future assessment impact studies in the area and also enable integration of all other assessment studies carried out in the vicinity. Through such a process it will be possible to evolve a national database of assessment studies which, in turn, will facilitate refinement of National Hazard and Vulnerability Mapping.
  - o Assessment of vulnerability against a hazard of a given magnitude should be carried out. The vulnerability of an individual or a group of individuals or of any element or an infrastructure like a flyover or a bridge, for a hazard of a given magnitude, will vary from 0 to 1 depending on the degree of mitigation built into the design. For example, an earthquake of magnitude 7 on the Richter

scale may render very unsafe school children in a poorly built school (vulnerability-1) whereas the residents of an earthquake-resistant neighbouring house for the same magnitude of earthquake, may be safe (vulnerability = 0). This distinction is essential because existence of hazard does not automatically mean vulnerability, and vulnerability does not necessarily have to be 1. The question of vulnerability has to be considered not only in a physical sense but in a comprehensive sense. Vulnerability could be physical, social, ecological, organizational, educational, attitudinal, political, cultural, or economical. Vulnerability assessment may also take note of medical care and casualty management that would be possible in the vicinity in case of natural or man-made disaster.

- Assessment of risk against a given hazard will be a function of hazard and vulnerability.
- Identification of elements at risk like population, properties, economic activities, public services, is to be brought out. By overlaying the infrastructure map of an area on the corresponding hazard map of the same scale, elements at risk can be identified.
- Particularly while carrying out hazard identification and risk assessment for industrial estates, issues like release scenario, consequences in terms of heat generation over pressure and toxicities, identification of hazardous chemicals, processes and operations, identification of important receptors, both environmental and physical, classification of units which have potential for creating an off-site emergency, and so on, need to be addressed.

The reliability of hazard, vulnerability, and risk

assessments will depend upon the quality of maps and other investigational data and various uncertainties involved due to inadequacy of data and other factors. It is therefore important that all major stages of project/scheme development, namely, planning, site investigations and designs, are subject to a process of rigorous peer review and accordingly certified.

Where projects specifically identified and designed for disaster management are to be appraised, the following factors would need to be considered:

- The proposed project or scheme (i) is to be need-based and demand driven; (ii) must fall within the high priority bracket, linked with the development plan of the area; (iii) should have well stipulated goals, clearly identified stakeholders and beneficiaries; (iv) should be fully backed with analyses of risks and quantified benefits in terms of disaster safety; and (v) should clearly reflect implications of not taking up the project in terms of disaster related risks, environmental protection, and economic development.
- Projects/schemes which yield multiplier effect for the greatest good of the largest number will deserve priority. For example, a well drafted practical disaster emergency plan for a school or disaster management plan for a district can inspire other schools and districts to yield the snow-balling (multiplier) effect. Similarly, development of a knowledge-based, multi-media disaster mitigation product when translated in different vernacular languages may at once multiply benefits.
- Project merit rating should also depend on the following factors:
    - o Breaking new ground in terms of scientific, technological or management innovation. including peoples' participation. For instance, development of an innovative early warning system against a particular type of disaster using simple, readily monitored indicators.

- o Delivering 'Best Practices' for others to emulate and getting inspired by them. For example, best practices of engineered constructions in a given earthquake-affected hilly area.
- o Choice of appropriate technology. For example, partially prefabricated construction technology will be more appropriate than the cast-in-place construction technology in a post-disaster reconstruction programme in a given situation.
- o Employment generation. For example, a judicious man-machine mix in the construction of flood prevention works may help generate employment in an area without unduly compromising on efficiency of work.
- o Sustainable capacity building. It is the key to empowering a village, district, State, or a region so that each one of them can, as far as possible, manage their own affairs in the event of a disaster. For example, water sampling and testing capacity at local level when post-disaster situations threaten epidemics.
- o Pro-active engagement of communities and spreading the culture of safety in communities and other levels. Disaster education and community leadership development, public awareness development, gender mainstreaming, special focus on the needs of women and children, vocational training of unemployed youth, and concern for physically challenged persons will add weight to the project/scheme.

- Since disasters know no district or State boundaries, projects of interest to two or more districts or States may score over those yielding localized benefits. By the same logic, national level mission-mode projects/schemes should get preference over others.

Financial Provisions for Disaster Management

It is important that a portion of the Plan funds is earmarked for efforts that directly or indirectly help in disaster management. Ideally, each project should provide adequately for the disaster mitigation and management expenditure that is identified by the appraisal process described in the previous section as being necessary. In addition, Central and State Governments may, depending upon their own hazard assessments, earmark a suitable and adequate amount for disaster mitigation schemes that are implemented over a definite time period.

The projects to be taken up should include:

- All schemes for generating basic input data for hazard and vulnerability impact analysis.
- Stand-alone disaster management projects such as mitigation projects, awareness programmes, capacity building projects, community-based disaster management projects, upgrading early warning systems, failsafe disaster management communication network, micro-zoning, and so on.
- Mainstreaming disaster reduction into already approved projects in sectors of education, housing, infrastructure, urban development, and the like. For example, projects already under implementation such as the SSA, which caters to the construction of school buildings, could be reviewed. The design of the school building under the programme could include hazard resistant features, at least in multi-hazard prone (earthquake, cyclone, flood), high-risk areas so that these are safe. Similarly, existing infrastructure like bridges and roads will need to be strengthened and upgraded to mitigate disaster at a subsequent stage.

Schemes/Programmes Identified/Proposed to be taken up in the Eleventh Five Year Plan

National level initiatives/projects for disaster management, identified and recommended by the Working

Group on Disaster Management and the NDMA for being taken up during the Eleventh Five Year Plan are indicated at Annexure 1.3. However, details of these projects/schemes will have to be worked out through preparation of project reports. Thereafter, such schemes as are approved for implementation during the Eleventh Five Year Plan will have to be accommodated within the sectoral allocations of the ministries concerned.

Apart from the projects/schemes mentioned above, a number of ongoing and proposed schemes of various ministries and departments of the GoI have a direct or indirect bearing on disaster management as these add to preparedness for responding to disasters or constitute the efforts towards recovery from the impact of disasters. Similarly, many developmental projects/schemes take care of the vulnerability to different kinds of disasters and provide for mitigation of their effects.

ANNEXURE 1.1

Financial Performance in the Tenth Plan

S. No.	Schemes/Programmes	Financial Performance Tenth Plan (Rs. in crore)			
		Outlay	BE	RE	Actual Exp.
1	2	3	4	5	6
1.	Central Pollution Control Board (CPCB)	100.00	147.90	138.90	140.06
2.	Industrial Pollution Abatement through Preventive Strategies	5.00	4.60	4.48	1.48
3.	Common Effluent Treatment Plants (CETP)	25.00	20.27	20.25	20.10
4.	Environmental Management in Heritage Pilgrimage and Tourism Centres, including Taj Protection	170.00	59.02	25.03	25.00
5.	Establishment of Environment Protection Authorities and Environment Commission and Tribunal	15.00	18.80	18.22	13.83
6.	Assistance for Abatement of Pollution and Environment Policy and Law	19.67	21.00	24.69	25.00
7.	Environmental Health	10.00	2.00	0.05	1.03
8.	Clean Technologies	25.00	12.50	9.19	5.18
9.	Environmental Impact Assessment (EIA)	13.00	11.80	11.07	12.35
10.	Industrial Pollution Prevention Project (EAP)	10.00	10.00	13.54	13.55
11.	Hazardous Substances Management	70.00	37.00	32.91	30.71
12.	Botanical Survey of India (BSI)	85.00	61.50	49.54	47.89
13.	Zoological Survey of India (ZSI)	45.00	49.37	50.87	45.51
14.	G.B. Pant Institute of Himalayan Environment and Development	35.00	34.00	36.96	37.00
15.	Biosphere Reserves	35.00	37.20	37.87	36.62

16.	Conservation and Management of Mangroves, Coral Reefs, and Wetlands	54.00	55.00	57.55	57.11
17.	Assistance of Botanical Gardens	15.00	9.50	7.25	6.96
18.	Biodiversity Conservation	12.00	15.00	17.00	15.51
19.	Taxonomy Capacity Building Project	10.00	8.50	8.34	8.96
20.	Institute of Biodiversity	16.00	1.00	0.00	0.00
21.	Research and Development	24.00	20.07	20.83	20.78
22.	Environment Education, Training, and Awareness	125.00	143.00	125.25	118.16
23.	National Museum of Natural History (NMNH)	40.00	31.50	28.56	26.71
24.	Centres of Excellence	45.00	38.00	36.56	33.28
25.	Environmental Information System (ENVIS)	14.00	17.50	20.03	19.55
26.	National Natural Resource Management System (NNRMS)	7.00	23.50	22.50	22.74
27.	Environment Management Capacity Building Project (EMCB) (EAP)	48.98	80.00	48.29	46.14
28.	Indo-Canada Environment Facility (ICEF) (EAP)	35.00	0.05	0.04	0.00
29.	GoI-UNDP-CCF Programme (EAP)	3.00	13.00	9.50	9.06
30.	Global Environment Facility (EAP)	0.05	0.01	0.01	0.00
31.	International Co-operation Activities	8.00	9.20	9.92	10.13
32.	Canada Assisted Centre for Excellence in Environmental Science, Technology, and Policy (EAP)	1.00	0.11	0.02	0.00
33.	Indo-German Technical Co-operation Project (EAP)	6.00	0.50	0.01	0.00
34.	State of Environment Project	6.00	6.15	7.26	6.26
35.	Information Technology (IT)	25.00	46.75	29.96	29.69
36.	Adaptation and Capacity Building Project on Climate Change (ACPCC)	30.00	21.83	28.05	26.99
37.	Strengthening of Plan Coordination	0.30	0.06	0.01	0.00
38.	Civil Construction Unit (CCU)	12.00	8.96	9.71	8.75

(Contd.)

ANNEXURE 1.1 *(Contd.)*

1	2	3	4	5	6
NEW SCHEMES					
39.	EPCO-Madhya Pradesh and Strengthening Natural Resource Management and Farmers Livelihood in Nagaland (EAP)		1.59	0.94	0.90
40.	Strengthening of Environment Information Centre		0.10	0.00	0.00
41.	National Coastal Management Programme		0.10	0.00	0.00
42.	Capacity building EIA and Revised Environmental Clearance Process		0.10	0.00	0.00
43.	Promotion of Bilateral Cooperation		0.00	0.00	0.00
	Total Environment	1200.00	1078.04	961.16	919.99
44.	NRCD	33.00	27.00	27.00	24.35
45.	NRCP	1342.00	1199.96	12.07.27	1134.89
46.	NRCP (EAP)	75.00	337.00	185.76	218.91
47.	NLCP	220.00	250.00	202.37	164.62
	Total NRCD	1670.00	1813.96	1622.40	1542.77

FORESTRY & WILDLIFE

48.	Indian Council for Forestry Research and Education (ICFRE)	210.00	226.86	228.57	227.95
49.	Grant-In-Aid to Indian Plywood Industries Research and Institute (IPIRTI)	10.00	12.10	14.20	14.15
50.	Indian Institute of Forest Management (IIFM)	20.00	21.00	22.77	12.46
51.	Training to IFS Officers	6.00	6.75	6.25	5.94
52.	Indira Gandhi National Forest Academy (ICNFA)	30.00	27.25	26.68	23.61
53.	Directorate of Forestry Education (DFE)	10.00	11.73	12.69	15.06
54.	Gregarious flowering of Muli (Melocanna baccifera) Bamboos		60.00	43.00	42.82
55.	Forest Survey of India (FSI)	35.00	29.50	26.97	27.15
56.	Integrated Forest Protection Scheme	445.00	279.84	224.47	208.01
57.	Strengthening of Forestry Divisions	34.00	31.50	32.94	33.79
58.	Afforestation through PRIs (NCMP-related scheme)	0.00	0.10	0.10	0.00
59.	Strengthening of Wildlife Divisions and outside Protected Areas	10.00	15.00	14.51	11.23
60.	Development of National Parks and Sanctuaries	350.00	230.50	240.11	234.65
61.	Wildlife Institute of India (WII)	50.00	45.00	49.47	46.07
62.	National Zoological Parks (NZP)		2.50	4.80	4.37
63.	Project Tiger				
64.	Biodiversity Conservation and Rural Livelihood Improvement Project (EAP)		4.00	3.33	2.03
65.	Eco-development around Protected Areas (EAP)	45.00	80.25	58.05	56.59
66.	Project Elephant	60.00	67.25	66.00	63.83

(Contd.)

ANNEXURE 1.1 (*Contd.*)

1	2	3	4	5	6
67.	Central Zoo Authority (CZA)	75.00	76.00	83.85	86.38
68.	Protection of Wildlife outside Protected Areas	60.00	10.11	0.01	0.00
	Total Forests & Wildlife	1600.00	1386.24	1319.73	1287.53
69.	Animal Welfare	175.00	70.50	81.02	75.22
	NAEB				
70.	National Afforestation and Eco-development Board (NAEB)	80.00	106.00	86.19	71.60
71.	National Afforestation Project (NAP)	1115.00	1224.10	1164.42	1179.02
72.	National Action Programme to Combat Desertification	30.00	3.00	0.02	0.00
73.	Eco-development Forces	75.00	42.00	41.04	42.96
	Total NAEF	1300.00	1375.10	1291.67	1293.63
	Grand Total	5945.00	5723.84	5275.98	5119.14

Source: Ministry of Environment and Forest (MOEF).

ANNEXURE 1.2

Physical Performance of Important Plan Schemes of the Tenth Plan

S. No.	Schemes/Programmes	Physical Performance	
		Targets	*Achievements*
1	2	3	4
1.	Central Pollution Control Board (CPCB)	National Ambient Air Quality Monitoring Program (NAMP)	Ambient air quality monitoring at 321 locations; water quality monitoring at 1019 locations.
2.	Environmental Management in Heritage Pilgrimage and Tourism Centres including Taj Protection		Moratorium due to court case.
3.	Clean Technologies	Life Cycle Assessment (LCA) studies and demonstration projects	Ten projects on Clean Technologies for food preservation, arsenic removal, bio-remediation of lakes, recycling of marble slurry, development of natural dyes; adhesives from forest waste; development of bamboo composites; utilization of anode muds and chips; air pollution control package for medium-scale lime kilns and development of eco-friendly welding machines.
4.	Hazardous Substances Management	Management of chemical emergoencies and hazardous substances	6 TSDFs set-up.
5.	Environment Education, Training and Awareness	Assistance to 100000 eco-clubs and 10000 organizations	33778 eco-clubs created (total 91378); 9784 organizations.

(Contd.)

ANNEXURE 1.2 (*Contd.*)

1	2	3	4
6.	National River Conservation Plan (NRCP)	Projects for 34 polluted river stretches in 160 towns for treating 5435 MLD sewage.	308 projects completed; creating treatment capacity for 2055 MLD sewage.
7.	National Lake Conservation Plan	Conservation of 35 lakes, 28 projects	Approved works in 42 new lakes; projects for 10 lakes completed.
8.	Indian Council for Forestry Research and Education (ICERE)	Co-ordinating research, education in institutes/universities	414 research projects initiated; 23 universities supported.
9.	Integrated Forest Protection Scheme	Assistance to States and UTs for identified activities	Assistance for fire protection (196819 kin) and forest boundary (219418 nos.) consolidation.
10.	Development of National Parks and Sanctuaries	Assistance to States and UTs for national parks and sanctuaries (total 606)	Assistance to 342 national parks and sanctuaries being provided.
11.	Project Tiger	Funding support to 28 Tiger Reserves	Funding support to 28 Tiger Reserves covered in the area of 37761 sq km.
12.	Project Elephant	Assistance to 15 States for elephant conservation.	Funds released for 25 Elephant Reserves in 15 States.
13.	Central Zoo Authority (CZA)	Assistance for management of zoos	293 zoos evaluated; 42 supported.
14.	Animal Welfare	Animal Welfare Board and construction of National Institute of Animal Welfare.	Animal Welfare Board and National Institute of Animal Welfare functioning.
15.	National Afforestation and Eco-development Board (NAEB)	Evaluation of projects and assistance to NGOs for afforestation.	650 projects evaluated.
16.	National Afforestation Project (NAP)	Afforestation project-based assistance to JFMCs.	729 projects involving 6.45 lakh ha in 29 States taken up.
17.	Eco-development Forces	Support to 4 Eco Task Force battalions.	4 Eco Task Force battalions supported.

Source: MOEF.

ANNEXURE 1.3

Projects/Schemes Identified by the Working Group/NDMA for being taken up by NDMA/MHA for Implementation during the Eleventh Plan

S. No.	*Name of the Project/Programme/Scheme*	*Objective*
1	*2*	*3*
1.	National Cyclone Risk Mitigation Project (with World Bank Assistance)	For mitigating hazard risks in the country & enhancing capabilities at various levels.
2.	National Earthquake Risk Mitigation Project	Strengthening structural & non-structural earthquake mitigation efforting and reducing risk and vulnerability in high risk districts.
3.	National Flood Mitigation Project	Multi-objectives including effective preparedness and improved promptness and capability, strengthening community capacity, and reduction in consequences of floods.
4.	National Landslide Mitigation Project	Strengthen the structural and non-structural landslide mitigation efforts and reduce the landslide risk and vulnerability in the hilly districts prone to landslides and mudflows.
5.	Expanded Disaster Risk Mitigation Project	Strengthen the structural and non-structural disaster preparedness and mitigation efforts to reduce the risk and vulnerability in the disaster-prone districts with community participation.
6.	National Disaster Communication Network (NDCN)	Dedicated communication & IT support for pro-active disaster support functions including for early warning and forecasting.
7.	Information, Education, and Communication (IEC) Programme	Disaster risk and vulerability reduction, disaster preparedness, structural and non-structural mitigation efforts and disaster response by developing ICT materials, print and electronic

(Contd.)

ANNEXURE 1.3 *(Contd.)*

1	2	3
		media products, campaigns, exhibitions, etc.
8.	Micro-zonation of Major Cities	To carry out micro-zonation of High Risk Cities in Seismic Zones IV and V to prepare strategies to reduce earthquake risk and vulnerability in the high risk districts.
9.	Project Preparation Facility/Research Programme Studies	Take up mitigation projects for disaster risk reduction and also undertake special studies and research programmes.
10.	Vulnerability Assessment Schemes	Gujarat has undertaken vulnerability analysis of different parts of the State to different forms of disasters. Such an analysis is urgently required to be carried out by other States too.
11.	International Co-operation	India needs to adopt a proactive approach for providing necessary support to the neighbouring countries through multilateral co-operation and involvement of regional organizations.
12.	Infrastructure of 8 NDRF Battalions	Completely new infrastructure has to be built for 6 battalions @ Rs. 80 crore per bn and existing infrastructure has to be upgraded for the 2 battalions @ Rs. 25 crore per bn.
13.	Upgradation of NIDM and other Institutes	The institute requires space and equipments for state-of-the-art emergency operations centre, disaster mitigation workshop, mock drill exercise, library, GIS laboratory, etc.

ANNEXURE 1.4

Tenth Plan Outlay and Actual Expenditure in Environment and Forest Sectors (States and UTs)

(Rs. lakh)

S. No.	State/UT	State Plan Outlay	Forestry & Wildlife			Ecology & Environment		
			Projected Outlay	Agreed Outlay	Actual Expenditure	Projected Outlay	Agreed Outlay	Actual Expenditure
1	2	3	4	5	6	7	8	9
1.	Andhra Pradesh	4661400	123779	113262.86	80076.85	620	203.72	316.29
2.	Arunachal Pradesh	388832	7700	9529.87	8403.42	42	208.91	38.46
3.	Assam	831522	7736	11235	9076.1	65	79	29.45
4.	Bihar	2100000	4514	7953.92	6267.25	0	0	0
5.	Chhattisgarh	1100000	32718	39180	46844.04	783	679.5	370.13
6.	Goa	320000	2500	2908.95	2880.93	300	795.45	799.33
7.	Gujarat	4000700	93634	75445.7	66076.37	2766	2196	1010.44
8.	Haryana	1028500	12733	32125	30612.03	283	407	277.46
9.	Himachal Pradesh	1030000	42377	36748.49	36344.2	50	27	82.59
10.	Jammu & Kashmir	1450000	36358	23794.13	23096.74	3619	465.42	288.4987

(Contd.)

ANNEXURE 1.4 *(Contd.)*

1	2	3	4	5	6	7	8	9
11.	Jharkhand	1463274	46277	49802	46875.73	0	0	0
12.	Karnataka	4355822	73396	51408.83	46677.84	1285	5535	2417.584
13.	Kerala	2400000	175000	22789	21348.75		0	0
14.	Madhya Pradesh	2618993	35275	64458.82	81330.29	5112	9663.63	8388..896
15.	Maharashtra	6663200	68279	10997.81	10729	1200	627.71	500
16.	Manipur	280400	1744	3704.66	3560.81	495	1714	556.75
17.	Meghalaya	300900	5250	6596	6093.89	275	300	174.34
18.	Mizoram	230001	2846	4285	4515.88	19	20	11.04
19.	Nagaland	222765	2250	2535	2828.24	100	178	272
20.	Orissa	1900000	69446	22899.95	6083.94	2030	2482.29	2561.30.5
21.	Punjab	1865700	28075	40800.6	30500.46	572	203.1	26.08
22.	Rajasthan	2731800	115320	52592.87	31584.73	464	100.95	35.8972
23.	Sikkim	165574	3500	3564.2	3510.45	600	160	125.97
24.	Tamilnadu	4000000	134810	63561.93	64601.18	11305	1578.16	486.2261
25.	Tripura	450000	4835	4273.65	4113.03	446	209	243.3501
26.	Uttar Pradesh	5970800	120800	49784	48642.5	235525	24979	2628.58

27. Uttaranchal	763000	20693	56223.18	62063.17	5902	2900	1505
28. West Bengal	2864100	16443	12908.12	6823.73	1688	1259.99	2487.03
Total (States)	56157283	1130788	875369.54	791561.55	275446	56972.83	25643.7
UTs							
29. Andaman & Nicobar	248300	7243	6369	6097.71	0	40	32.88
30. Chandigarh	100000	1733	2455	1916	270	323	188.13
31. Dadra & Nagar Haveli	30400	1200	1657	1733.87	0	0	0
32. Daman & Diu	24500	278	200	173.38	0	5	13.1
33. Delhi	2300000	2600	2300	14791.16	4800	2705	998.6
34. Lakshadweep	43700	92.3	91.7	46	400.3	163.3	102.52
35. Pondicherry	190649	500	859	819.54	176	244	257.13
Total (UTs)	2937549	13646.3	13931.7	25577.66	5646.3	3480.3	1592.38
Total (States/UTs)	59094832	11444343	889301.24	817139.21	281092.3	60453.13	27236.08
Percentage to Total	100	1.94	1.50	1.38	0.48	0.10	0.05

ANNEXURE 1.5

State-wise and Scheme-wise Releases of Central Funds to Ongoing CSS under MoEF during the Tenth Plan

Name of the State/Scheme	*CETPs*	*Indus. Polln. Preven-tion*	*Taj Protec-tion*	*Bio-sphere Reserve*	*Man-groves, Coral Reefs & Wetlands*	*NRCP*	*NLCP*	*Tigher Project*	*India Eco-Dev. Project*	*Project Ele-phant*	*IFPS*	*Dev. of National Parks and Sanc-tuaries*	*NAP*	*Gre-gari-ous Flow-ering*	*Total 2000-07*
1	*2*	*3*	*4*	*5*	*6*	*7*	*8*	*9*	*10*	*11*	*12*	*13*	*14*	*15*	*16*
Andhra Pradesh	0.30	3.24			1.20	115.8	0.80	1.74		2.78	6.94	4.91	53.18		190.94
Arunachal Pradesh				1.13	0.00			5.49		3.05	10.34	5.91	14.18	0.75	40.84
Assam				0.89	2.88			3.15		4.95	11.67	8.24	33.07	3.25	68.10
Bihar						0.66		2.36			3.93	3.80	0.35	12.98	24.09
Chhattisgarh		1.58						2.65		0.64	12.08	13.53	44.95		75.03
Goa					1.20	8.56					0.99	0.93	0.64		12.33
Gujarat	4.28	1.01			8.40	42.54			13.67		9.46	9.71	48.80		137.87
Haryana						16.78				0.50	5.11	1.73	40.99		65.12
Himachal Pradesh					1.41						3.70	11.52	38.89		55.53
Jammu & Kashmir					2.26			70.00			3.78	5.89	31.01		112.94
Jharkhand								5.77	4.48		8.08	3.86	46.15		68.33
Karnataka		4.38		2.73	3.07	31.48	22.93	16.07	10.42	7.65	4.55	28.05	101.2		232.95
Kerala				3.64	2.18	0.75	4.30	5.61	2.35	8.07	7.51	12.73	25.09		72.23
Madhya Pradesh		1.21		3.78	0.30	39.90	4.58	41.47	8.56		11.93	21.82	71.08		204.63
Maharashtra	15.24				57.93	66.73	5.50	17.46		0.25	3.03	9.07	64.93		237.14
Manipur					0.86						6.78	4.31	26.99	5.44	44.39

Meghalaya				1.34						2.67	2.30	3.16	13.45	1.71	24.62
Mizoram				0.25			4.66		0.05	17.94	11.40	65.47	13.33	110.10	
Nagaland									2.20	12.81	2.01	35.64	6.32	58.98	
Orissa				2.53	6.53	28.99	1.21	5.92		5.85	4.27	13.07	67.54		135.91
Punjab					1.88	88.40					1.01	0.03	10.17		101.49
Rajasthan	0.37			2.04	0.44	15.00	9.86	8.64		2.70	12.28	27.69		79.02	
Sikkim				2.64		1.79					6.82	5.75	27.80		44.80
Tamil Nadu	0.11			1.81	6.86	480.30	0.73	4.85		5.38	8.14	8.37	76.53		593.08
Tripura							0.50	0.50		0.36	10.40	4.28	21.36	11.32	48.61
Uttar Pradesh			0.24		1.00	121.07	1.49	7.37		0.18	5.61	12.25	89.01		238.22
Uttaranchal				3.50	0.42	20.02	31.94	9.12		6.10	13.37	4.28	44.41		133.00
West Bengal				3.52	7.53	135.53	5.11	9.10	4.14	6.97	8.45	14.26	27.79		222.42
Total States	19.93	11.79	0.24	27.50	108.21	1192.82	164.09	153.16	52.26	64.58	203.58	233.70	1154.91	42.12	3432.88
Union Territories															
Andaman & Nicobar				2.50	0.83							2.11			5.45
Chandigarh				0.85								0.14			1.09
Dadra and Nagar Haveli											0.52	0.70			1.22
Delhi						121.25						0.20			121.45
Lakshadweep					0.30										0.30
Total UTs				3.45	1.13	121.25					0.52	3.15			129.50
Total States/UTs	19.93	11.79	0.24	30.95	109.34	1321.07	164.09	153.16	52.26	61.58	204.10	236.84	1154.91	42.12	3562.38

Source: MOEF.

Bibliography

A Survey of Research in Public Administration, 1980-90.

Abbasi, S.A., Hot Topics: Everyday Environmental Concerns.

Alex, Jacob P., Disaster Management: Towards a Legal Framework.

All India Symposium on Drought Prone Areas of India (Tirupati: Jan. 16, 1978). Proceedings by All India Symposium on drought prone areas of India, Tirupati: S.Y. University, Department of Geography, 1977, 322 p. Organised by Sri Venkateswara University, Department of Geography.

Anderson, Mary B., The Nepal 1988 Earthquake: Environment and Natural Disaster Management.

Awaradi, S.A., Disaster Management Plan for Andaman and Nicobar Islands.

Bhargava, Gopal, Environmental Challenges and Ecological Disaster:

Global Perspective by Gopal Bhargava, New Delhi: Mittal, 1992, 247 p.

Bhatia, B.M., Famines in India: A Study in some aspects of the Economic History of India with special references to food problem, 1980-81 by B.M. Bhatia, Delhi: Konar, 1991, 383 p.

Brainstorming Session on Management of Drought, 2002 (September 13, 2003: Indian Institute of Public Administration, New Delhi): Papers.

Building Safer Cities: The Future of Disaster Risk.

Carter, T. Michael, Before Disaster Strikes: Plan for Humanitarian Assistance, H.R. Focus, Dec. 91, pp. 3-4.

Carter, W. Nick, Disaster Management: A Disaster Manager's Handbook, Chawla, K.L., Disaster Management-Flood Control: A Study in Cost Benefit Analysis.

Conference and Trade Show on Abstracts for the Pan Pacific Hazards (July 29-August 2, 1996: Vancouver, B.C.): Proceedings.

Dandekar, Y.M., A Survey of Famine Conditions in the affected Areas of Maharashtra and Mysore by V.M. Dandekar and Vasant P. Pethe, Poona: Gokhale Institute of Politics and Economics, 1972, 203 p. (Gokhale Institute mimeograph series No. 13).

David, Hizabeth and Judith Mayer, Comparing costs of alternative flood hazard mitigation plans: The case of soldiers grove, Wisconsijl, Journal of the American Planning Association, 50 (1), Winter 1984, pp. 22-23.

Disaster Mitigation in Asia and the Pacific by Asian Development Bank,

Manila, ADB, 1991, 392 p.

Disaster Resilient Infrastructure.

District Disaster Management Plan, Aizawl.

Dr. Vinod K. Sharma, India Disaster Management.

Final Report of Australia's Coordination for the International Decade for Natural Disaster Reduction, 1990-2000.

Gauriar, Santosh, Natural Disaster Management with Emphasis on Flood Management.

Goel, S.L., Administration of Personnel in Co-operative (New Delhi, 1979), Sterling Publishers (Co-Author B.B. Goel), Health Care Administration: Ecology, Principles and Modern Trends (New Delhi, 1980), Sterling Publishers, Health Care Administration: Policy-making and Planning (New Delhi, 1980), Sterling Publishers.

——, Advanced Public Administration (New Delhi, 1993), Sterling Publishers, Development Planning and Administration (ed.) S. Bhatnagar (Co-editor) (New Delhi, 1992), Deep and Deep Publications.

——, Distance Education in 21st Century, New Delhi, March 2000, Deep and Deep Publications.

——, Education Policy and Administration (New Delhi, 1994), Deep and Deep Publications.

Goel, S.L., Encyclopaedia of Disaster Management.

——, Financial Administration and Management (New Delhi, 1993), Sterling Publishers.

——, Health Care Administration: Levels and Aspects (New Delhi, 1980), Sterling Publishers.

——, Hospital Administration and Management (ed.) Co-Author Dr. R. Kumar in 3 Volumes (New Delhi, 1989), Deep and Deep Publications.

——, International Administration: WHO South-East Asia Regional Office (New Delhi, 1977), Sterling Publishers, Principles, Problems and Prospects of Co-operative Administration (New Delhi, 1979), Sterling Publishers (Co-Author Dr. B.B. Goel).

——, Modern Management Techniques (New Delhi, 1990), Deep and Deep Publications (Revised & Reprinted, International Civil Service: Principles, Problems and Prospects) (New Delhi, 1984), Sterling Publishers.

——, Personnel Administration and Management (New Delhi, 1993), Sterling Publishers.

——, Policy and Administration: Family Planning & Beyond (New Delhi, 1990), Deep and Deep Publications.

——, Primary Health Care Administration in 21st Century, Principles, Ecology and Features, Deep & Deep Publications Pvt. Ltd., 2000.

——, Primary Health Care Administration in 21st Century: Health Programmes and Activities, Deep & Deep Publications Pvt. Ltd., 2000.

——, Primary Health Care Administration in 21st Century: Managerial Issues, Deep and Deep Publications Pvt. Ltd., 2000.

——, Primary Health Care Administration in 21st Century: Organisational Set-up from Village to International Level, Deep & Deep Publications Pvt. Ltd., 2000.

——, Public Health Administration (New Delhi, 1984), Sterling Publishers.

——, Public Personnel Administration, (New Delhi, 1984), Reprint, 1987, Sterling Publishers.

——, Social Welfare Administration, Vols. I and II: Theory

and Practice (New Delhi, 1988), Deep and Deep Publications (Co-Author Dr. R.K. Jain).

Goel, S.L., Disaster Administration and Management, Text and Case Studies, New Delhi, Deep & Deep, 2007.

——, Encychopaedea of Disaster Administration, 3 Volumes, New Delhi, Deep & Deep, 2006.

Goel, S.L. and Ram Kumar, Disaster Management, Deep and Deep Publication, Pvt. Ltd., 2001.

Green Paper on Disaster Management.

Health Sector Contingency Plan for Management of Crisis Situations in India.

IIPA: Natural Disaster Rehabilitation Housing and Structural Mitigation and Case Study for Earthquake Affected Areas by India Disaster Management Training Country Workshop (July 12-16, 1993: New Delhi).

India: Disaster Management Training Country Workshop (1993, 12-16 July: PA: New Delhi), Introduction to Hazard.

India: Disaster Management Training Country Workshop (1993,12-16 July: IIPA: New Delhi): Overview of Disaster Management.

India: Disaster Management Training Country Workshop (1993, 12-16 July: IIPA: New Delhi): Disaster Economics.

India: Disaster Management Training Country Workshop (1993, 12-16 July: IIPA: New Delhi): Vulnerability and Risk Assessment.

India: Disaster Management Training Country Workshop (1993, 12-16 July: IIPA, New Delhi): Disaster Mitigation.

India: Disaster Management Training Country Workshop (1993, 12-16 July: IIPA, New Delhi): Disaster Assessment. ..

India: Disaster Management Training Country Workshop (1993, July 12-16: IIPA, New Delhi): Disaster Preparedness.

India: Disaster Management Training Country Workshop (1993, July 12-16: IIPA, New Delhi): Displaced Persons in Civil Conflict.

India: Disaster Management Training Country Workshop

(1993, July 12-16: IIPA, New Delhi): Disaster and Development.

India: Disaster Management Training Country Workshop (July 11-16, 1993: New Delhi), Disaster Assessment.

India: Disaster Management Training Country Workshop on Disaster Assessment (July 12-16, 1993): Proceedings.

India: High Powered Committee on Disaster Management: The Report of the High Powered Committee on Disaster Management.

India: High Powered Committee on Disaster Management: National Disaster Response Plan (Prepared by High Powered Committee on Disaster Management).

Informal Settlements, Environmental Degradation, and Disaster Vulnerability: The Turkey Case Study.

International Conference on Disaster Management: Cooperative Networking in South Asia (Nov. 28-30, 1999: New Delhi): Papers.

International Conference Series on Innovative Urban Community Development and Disaster Management (Sep. 26, 1995: Kyoto, Sep. 27-28, 1995: Osaka): Proceedings.

Kulshrestha, S.M., Drought Management in India and Potential Contribution of Climate Prediction.

Kulshrestha, S.M., Flood Management in India.

Lessons Learned from Community-based Flood Mitigation and Preparedness Project in Cambodia.

Living with Risk: A Global Review of Disaster Reduction Initiatives, Maharashtra Disaster Management Plan.

Man and Society in disaster edited by George W. Baker and Dwight W. Chapman, N.Y.: Basic Books, 1962, 442 p.

Managing Disaster Risk in Mexico: Market Incentives for Mitigation Investment.

Manual on Natural Disaster Management in India.

Mcalpin, Michel Burge, Subject of famine: Food crises and economic change in Western India, 1860-1920 by Michel Burge Mcalpin, J.E Princeton University Press, 1983, 288 p. Bibli., pp. 271-83.

Mehta, Aashil Kapur, Training Programme on Economic

Analysis and Disaster Management.

Mishra, V.K., Role of Armed Forces in Natural Disaster Management.

Moboisee, Roymond, M., Industrial Security for Strikes, Riot, Disasters by Raymond M. Moboisse, Springfield: C. Thomas, 1968, 496 p.

Modi, Jatin, Disaster Management, *Quarterly Journal of the All India Institute of Local Self-Government*; 10(3), July-Sept. 1989, p. 133.

Mutreja, S.K., Disaster Management: A Case Study of Earthquake Disaster in Gujarat Response to Crisis.

National Seminar on Disaster Management and Mitigation (20-21 June, 2003: Chennai): Proceedings of the 2003 National Seminar.

Natural Disaster Hotspots: Case Studies.

Natural Disaster Hotspots: A Global Risk Analysis.

Natural Disaster Management.

Natural Disasters and their Mitigation: A Remote Sensing and GIS Perspective.

Noson, Linda, Integrating Natural Hazards in the Planning Process, Risk Control Planning Workbook.

P. Kumar, Disaster Management in India: Need for an Integrated Approach.

PA Drought and Famine, Disaster Management Training Country Workshop, July 12-16, 1993, held at IIPA; New Delhi.

Paranjape, H.K., The Bhopal's Gas Disaster: A Chronology of Principal Events, in the Bhopal Gas Disaster Litigation, *Janta*, 46(34), 1 Dec., 1991, pp. 9-11.

Pollem, John D., Managing Catastrophic Disaster Risks: Using Alternative Risk Financing and Pooled Insurance Structures.

Post-disaster Damage Assessment and Need Analysis.

Prasad, J.K, Role of Non-governmental Organizations in Natural Disaster Management.

Project Completion Report of the Indonesian Urban Disaster Mitigation Project.

Project Completion Report of the Sri Lanka Urban Multi-hazard Disaster Mitigation Project.

Public Administration in the New Millennium: Challenges and Prospects.

Ramesh, K.S., Cyclone Disaster Management in Coastal District of Andhra Pradesh: A Case Study.

SAARC Workshop on Natural Disaster Reduction (March 30-April 2, 1994: New Delhi): Proceedings.

Sharma, Anil Kumar, Disaster Mitigation by Regulating Engineering Profession: A Legislative Framework.

Sharma, R.K., Role of farm extension in drought management by R.K Sharma, Delhi: Agricultural Economic Research Centre, Univ. of Delhi, 1990, p. 95.

Singh, Hulas, MDPA Dissertation on Development and Disaster Management.

Singh, K. Suresh, The Indian Famine 1967: A study in crises and change by K. Suresh Singh, New Delhi: People's Publishing House, 1975, 312 p.

Singh, Rajesh, Disaster Management Mechanism of Goa: A Critical Appraisal.

Singh, S.S., Legislative Framework for Disaster Management: A Study of Legislations in Select Countries.

Sinha, Anil, Culture of Prevention: Natural Disaster Management (India).

Sinha, Anil, Disaster Management: Lessons Drawn and Strategies for Future.

Siromony, P. Michael, Source Book on District Disaster Management.

Source Book on Disaster Management.

Strengthening Disaster Management, India.

Taori, Kamal, Disaster Management through Panchayati Raj.

The High Level Committee's Report on Disaster Management over Indian Railways: Proceedings.

The National Natural Disaster Reduction Plan of the People's Republic of China (1998-2010).

Tools and Resources for Post-disaster Relief.

Training Programme on Watershed Management in KBK-DPAP-IWDP Districts of Orissa (23rd-27th November, 1998: Bhubaneswar): Reading Materials.

United Nations' Economic and Social Commission for Enhancing Regional Cooperation in Infrastructure Development including that Related to Disaster Management.

Upadhyay, J.N., Role of Panchayati Raj Institutions in Disaster Management.

Uppal, J.N., Bengal famine of 1943; A man-made tragedy by J.N. Uppal, Delhi: Atma Ram, 1984, 269 p.

Verma, B.K., Disaster Management in India: A Community Perspective.

Visit of High Level Delegation led by Shri Sharad Pawar, MP and Vice-Chairman, National Committee on Disaster Management to Signapore, New Zealand and Australia: (30th March-13th April, 2002); Report.

White Paper on Disaster Management.

Workshop on "Disaster Management in the North-East Region: Floods and Earthquake" (June 28-29th, 2002; Guwahati); Report.

Workshop on Himalayan Eco-Development and Natural Disaster Reduction (Nov. 27-28, 1995; New Delhi), Proceedings.

Workshop on Urban Risk Reduction in Asia.

Yodmani, Suvit, Disaster Risk Management and Vulnerability Reduction: Protecting the Poor.

Index